COMMUNISM AND CHRISTIAN FAITH

Things and actions are what they are, and their consequence
will be what they will be: why then should we seek to b
deceived?

—Bishop Butler

Philosophers have previously offered various interpretations o
the world. Our business is to change it.

—Karl Marx

Calvinism was an active and radical force. It was a cree
which sought, not merely to purify the individual, but t
reconstruct Church and State, and to renew society by pene
trating every department of life, public as well as private, wit
the influence of religion.

—R. H. Tawney

To leave error unrefuted is to encourage intellectual immorality

—Karl Marx

Communism
& Christian Faith

By Lester DeKoster
Director of the Library
Calvin College and Seminary

William B. Eerdmans Publishing Co., Grand Rapids, Michigan

To Ruth

This volume is a redevelopment in considerably enlarged form of the thoughts expressed in a small book published in 1956 and now out of print, *All Ye That Labor.*

To the heads of Calvin College and Seminary, Presidents William Spoelhof and John Kromminga, go my hearty thanks for the creation of an atmosphere surrounding my vocation as librarian which encourages avocational efforts such as this one. For all that I owe to my mentor, critic, and friend, Dr. Henry J. Stob of Calvin Theological Seminary, mere words of thanks are hardly expressive enough. But he knows. And to my wife, and children, whom she daily taught to have patience with that far-off look in daddy's eyes when he did open the study door, I owe . . . well, this: without her — and them — nothing. . . .

The Publishers and their staff have been unfailingly patient and uncommonly helpful.

All told, God has been very good.

I can only wish that this book may so serve in the world as to be of some small return to all those I mention for all their goodness to me.

— LESTER DeKOSTER

CONTENTS

PREFACE   vii

INTRODUCTION   1

1. MARX AND MARXISM   7
   Karl Marx   7
   Marxism   11
   Proletariat and Bourgeoisie   13
   The Theory of Labor Value   14
   The Theory of Surplus Value   16
   The Fair Wage   20
   Class Struggle   22
   Economic Determinism   25
   Dialectical Materialism   28
   Revolution, Dictatorship, Paradise   31
   Summary   35

2. CAPITALISM, THE CLASSLESS SOCIETY, and MAN   36
   Basic Premises of Capitalism   36
   Capitalism and Criticism   39
   Marxist "Theology"   41
   Evil and Salvation in Marxism   43
   Stalinism   46
   The Classless Society   47
   Evil and Salvation in Christianity   51
   The Christian Doctrine of Property   54
   Christian Stewardship   57

3. HISTORY AND UTOPIA   63
   The Classless Society and History   64

Christianity and History   68
Marxist Utopianism and Real Society   69
Routes to Utopia   76

4. DIALECTICAL MATERIALISM   82
   Basic Assumptions   83
   Freedom, Necessity, and Mystery   84
   Man and Necessity   86
   God and Satan   92
   The Power of Negation   94
   Concluding Critique   97

5. LIBERALISM, MARXISM, AND CHRISTIANITY   100
   Contemporary Capitalism   100
   Classical Liberalism   103
   Christian Social Criticism   109
   A Christian Social Order   112

6. CHRISTIAN ANTI-COMMUNISM   119
   Serve the Truth   121
   Examine Self   124
   Discern the Real Enemy   129
   Love Your Enemies   133
   A Positive Program   136

7. ANTI-COMMUNISM BOOK LIST   140
   Introduction   141
   The Economic Background   142
   The Philosophic Background   142
   Karl Marx   143
   The Marxists   143
   The Russian Revolution   145
   Communism in America   147
   Anti-Communism   147
   Christianity and Communism   148
   A Christian Society   150

Bibliography   151

Indexes   155

A new titanism bestrides the globe and reaches for the moon. Communism is its name.

Why have so many flocked to its red banners? By what alchemy has it unlocked human hearts, released boundless human energies, and elicited untold human devotion and sacrifice?

These are crucial questions. They go, it seems to me, to the heart of the global conflict between Communism and . . . and What? What have we, Americans, Christians, who would be wholly anti-Communist, to match against Communism as a comparable, to say nothing of a superior, catalyst? Bluntly, what god do we, in fact — and what God must we in truth — two separate questions — oppose to this red god?

For the mysterious dynamic of history resides in man's choice of gods. In the service of his god — or gods (they may be legion) —a man expends his energies, commits his sacrifices, devotes his life. And history is made. Understand Communism, then, as a religion; or miss the secret of its power! Grasp the nature of this new faith, and discern in contrast to it the God who alone can oppose its onward march; or misapprehend the character of the contest in which mankind is engaged, and misconceive our own historic task.

These are the imperatives which obligate us to the study of Communism. And this study, if it is to be more than an intellectual holiday, is a study directed upon the dynamics of history — in order to influence their course, in order to harness upon them the pattern of a Christian society.

Marx was not, and had no desire to be, a conscious disciple of Jesus Christ. But the significant, fateful distinction Marx drew between those who study history only to *understand* it, and those who understand history in order to *change* it, is an

1

essentially Christian distinction, drawn long before Marx's time. Understanding as an *end in itself,* or communicated as an *end in itself,* is an idolatry, *not* the less so because more sophisticated than the worship of palpable idols of silver and stone, *not* the less so because it is able to masquerade as the end of man's highest and most distinctive faculty, his reason. The soul that seeks understanding as its ultimate good is embarked upon an infinite search with finite resources. Every new discovery is but labor and sorrow because it pushes farther away the tantalizing horizon; and Bali Ha'i — the island of heart's desire — never is won, nor can be. Unlike the rich fool, the scholarly idolator cannot even fill his barns — the measure of his greater foolishness. Idols, even the most respectable of them, never satisfy, not only; make their worshippers faintly contemptuous of their "lesser" fellows, not only; but deflect human energies fatally from the service of the true God. If Marx dared to call nineteenth-century man to understand history *in order to change* it, he but pervertedly obscured God's demand from out of history's beginning that men serve Him *through* understanding *in order that* the kingdom of God might come. Obedience, the Lord's Prophets demanded, *before* sacrifice; charity, the Lord's Son commanded, even *before* "Lord, Lord." If Marxists change history more these days than do the children of those who once "turned the world upside down," it is because Christians have idolatrously *subordinated* changing history to understanding (or otherwise enjoying) it; while the Marxists have it the other way around. Nor will the balance be likely to shift and the tide turn until Christians in this respect put their pleasures — even *intellectual* ones — at the disposal of the kingdom of God.

This small volume, whatever its many limitations, is not meant to be merely a map of Communist ideological landscape, fascinating as that might be. It is offered as a guide to landmarks specifically for purposes of *invasion,* intellectual indeed, but more than that, spiritual and practical. It is offered, too, as a challenge to Americans to define the gods we really serve in order to purge our service of all substitutes for the one, true God; and then to oppose by word and, above all, by deed, this true *service* to Communist *servitude.*

To approach this high goal, we must thoroughly *understand,* indeed, what Communist theory is; we must apprehend, too, the nature of those ends our society serves; and we must dedicate our energies ever more to the definition and realization of a

Christian society. While no doubt much of this understanding can be had from our easy chairs, neither our understanding nor we ourselves will matter much to history if we forget Leon Trotsky's tart warning: "Only a participant can be a profound spectator."

There is an urgency about these tasks, imposed upon us by the crisis of our times. For the Communist threat is a product of our own civilization, and this grotesque offspring nurtured by our historical sins threatens to destroy its father.

The crisis of our era has a double root: first, an inheritance is running out, and will, unless renewed, be soon dissipated; and second, debts are falling due. Together these threaten, in the form of Communism, our whole manner of life; and together they demand of us an heroic return to the true Source of our freedoms, and an heroic devotion to His demands upon our way of life in America, and upon America's way of life in the world.

First, the spiritual inheritance upon which our liberties are drawn was built up over the centuries out of a Christian appreciation of man; that is, man as created and sustained by God, and therefore obligated to serve Him above all and his neighbor as himself. This inheritance has, as Berdyaev argues in his *Meaning of History*, gradually been dissipated by three hundred years or more of a humanism deliberately estranging itself from its Root. "God, Sire," said LaPlace briskly to King Louis, "is unnecessary." "Then," the Monarch *might* have replied, "man is undone." That the king was gifted with no such foresight is a mark of his time and of its direction.

"Thus saith the Lord!" is normative for those who believe in the Lord; it is hardly mandatory for those who believe only in man. It may have taken Buchenwald and Siberia fully to illustrate this point; it may even take a third world war to drive it home to the survivors it leaves, if any. For man minus soul is only dust; and soul minus God is precisely an illusion, one with no "future" at all.

The gigantic liberations achieved by humanistic democracy, the force of which especially in America is happily by no means extinct, owe their accomplishment to an estimation of man inherited from a Christianity which this same humanism set itself long ago to explaining away — how effectively indeed may be observed from the *story* of philosophy: once a proud science of sciences, attuned to the reality of God; now mumbling unnoticed in corners about the meaning of its own symbols.

The American *Declaration of Independence* is the last significant political document which attributed human freedom to a superhuman source. Its immediate successor, the French *Declaration of the Rights of Man,* its title betraying already the shift of emphasis, ignores the Creator; and fifty years later, the *Communist Manifesto* sneers at Him. These tracts of the times accurately reflect the trends of the times.

But "Thus saith man!" is not, the record shows, calculated to make devils tremble.

Man was bent on making his own rights. Small wonder, then, if other generations of *men* chose to un-make them. The hideous brutalities of dictatorship were embryonic in the *Manifesto;* but was not the *Manifesto* seeded in the French *Declaration?* and was not that *Declaration* a gleam in the eye of the Renaissance? That a Puritan counter-current flowered in the American *Declaration* only delineates more clearly the direction of the main stream.

And now, an inheritance has been spent — or almost spent. Will it be renewed in our generation by an infusion from its Christian Source, or will liberty flicker out once more?

Because, in the second place, the debts are falling due, while the inherited wealth is eaten away. Debts created even as democracies were made, now are presented to democracies for payment. Colonialism and a proletariat sprang up alongside declarations of human rights, neither decisively affected by them. Peoples exploited and oppressed now rise to make these declarations and rights their own. They will wait no longer, envy no longer, grovel no longer. They demand their own 1776!

And who dons a mantle of feigned concern and promises payment? Who sits in the gate and offers to outdo his father? Who offers 1917 in lieu of 1776? The Communist monster!

The circle comes round. The child of a godless humanism now proposes to assume his father's obligations in order to destroy him. This is the nature of the crisis of our age.

The battle is joined — the new religion versus echoes of the old. The victory hangs upon a renascence of the old. It hangs upon the reestablishment of democracy upon its true foundation, as enunciated in the American *Declaration.* It hangs upon a personal and a national effort to actualize for all men, at home and abroad, the promises of the kingdom of God, in subservience to the one, only true King.

Who could have lived in times more challenging than these?

Let us ask, then, in the pages that follow, first what the theoretical structure of Communism, or Marxism (I shall use the terms synonymously) is. Next, let Marxism be subjected to criticism from a Christian perspective. And, finally, let us oppose to this false religion the "faith of our fathers, living still" as the gate to the future and the dynamic of a Christian society. All this as guide to action, each in his calling.

CHAPTER **1**

MARX AND MARXISM

KARL MARX made no bombs, carried no red flags, fought behind no street barricades . . . and died peacefully in his chair.

He was brilliant — so were others. He was learned — so were others. He was passionate — so were others. He lived most of his life in poverty — so did many. He was a genius, whatever that means exactly — there were more. What was it, then, that made this man unique, a secular prophet uncommonly persuasive? Steadfastly he denied mystery, but he was himself a mystery, as all men, especially men of genius, are. Already, before he formulated it, his own harsh materialism is breached — by himself. The phenomena of his life are quickly told; the secret of his power eludes us.

KARL MARX

This man was born in 1818. His parents were German citizens, of Jewish faith and race. They accepted Protestant Christianity, perhaps for reasons more material than spiritual, in 1824; and the whole family was baptized. Karl's later reaction to this event to which he was unwitting party is probably summarized in his vehement, "In a single word, I hate all gods."

There was little doubt of his brilliance almost from the beginning. He learned readily, criticized freely. He mastered law at Bonn University, history at Berlin, and philosophy at Jena. At age twenty-three he was granted at Jena the doctorate in philosophy; and already he was marked by the state and university authorities as tinged with radicalism.

His thesis at Jena was titled *The Difference Between the Natural Philosophy of Democritus and Epicurus*. No supernatural for him! And this "difference" he regarded all his life — if Democritus be the patron spirit of materialism, and Epi-

7

curus the god of those whose life consists in eating, drinking, and making merry.

The state controlled the universities, and Marx was suspect; therefore, no university career opened to the brilliant young graduate. Casting about under the restraint of official disgrace, which haunted him all his life, Dr. Marx found a job as reporter for a newspaper, the *Rheinische Zeitung* — call it the *Rhineland Gazette* — not exactly unknown to the Prussian censorship for its own liberal views.

In 1841 he was a reporter. In 1842 he was the editor. He so clearly demonstrated that the government's suspicions of him were not unfounded that before the end of 1843 the *Zeitung* was suspended and the Editor was on his way, by invitation, to exile in Paris. With him as his bride went his youthful sweetheart, the daughter of a member of Prussian officialdom, Jenny von Westphalen. Whether the Baron von Westphalen was enthusiastic about the match is open to question. That his daughter chose to share sunshine (of which, little enough) and shadow (of which, much) with the young outcast is early evidence of the strength she had, and needed, to sustain this uncommon marriage to the end. She died but fifteen months before Marx himself, after most of his work was done. After that he waited only to join her. But now his work was beginning.

In Paris, Marx made the acquaintance of Friedrich Engels, two years his junior and son of a wealthy English cotton-spinner. Eventually a harmony of mind developed between them which has indissolubly united their names. Engels accepted the status of protégé of the more vigorous personality and more original mind of Marx, but evidence of his own precise intellect appears in much of the work they did, whether pubished jointly or separately. Together they composed that most famous document, *The Communist Manifesto* of 1848, which sums up in highly rhetorical prose most of their ideology.

As some evidence of the stature of these two friends, it is instructive to note their pastimes. Engels dabbled in languages, and Marx in mathematics, for recreation. On one occasion Engels writes to Marx that he has allotted himself two weeks to master Persian. Presumably he succeeded. Marx might, had he cared, have carved himself a niche in the history of pure mathematics; but he had his eye on another Hall of Fame.

How Marx impressed those who admired him in his youthful cub reporter days is revealed by an ecstatic description penned of him by one Moses Hess, a colleague on the ill-starred *Zeitung.* Exulted Hess, "Imagine Rousseau, Voltaire, Holbach, Lessing, Heine and Hegel united in one person — I say united, not lumped together — and you have Dr. Marx." Well, imagine it for yourself; in terms of historical results, he did not miss by far.

In the hectic days of 1848, when revolution stalked the streets of Europe, Marx made his way back to Cologne and persuaded a group of liberals to found a *New Rhineland Gazette,* with Marx as editor. Once again his words stung officialdom, roused the restless, and in July, 1849, set the editor once more en route to exile. He arrived in London on August 24, 1849. He never left.

The British Museum, with its marvelous library and reading room where Marx soon established squatter's rights to a study table, became his base of operations. He ransacked the inexhaustible riches of books, documents, and reports, ever pressing toward the formulation of his "system," to be published at last as *Das Kapital,* of which only one volume appeared before his death. Of these sacred scriptures of Marxism — like other scriptures, more honored in word than in reading — three additional volumes followed posthumously. Two, edited by Engels, completed Marx's systematic work; the fourth, edited by Kautsky, added scattered writings. Its English title is simply, *Capital.*

The Marx family lived much of their English life in gruesome poverty, a living barely eked out by gifts from Engels, by slender returns from articles submitted to Horace Greeley's *New York Tribune,* and by repeated journeys to the pawnbroker with Jenny's heirlooms. Visitors to the Marx abode often stood rather than risk the rickety chairs; food was scant, and bill collectors many. Obliged to humble his natural pride by begging tidbits from friend and foe, sometimes confined to his bed for warmth or when his only suit was being cleaned or mended, this genius wrote his books and pamphlets with spiritual blood. He paid, and his family paid. Of six children, two died from malnutrition in their infancy, and a third shattered for a while the father's hold upon himself by his sudden death at eight. In all the squalor and confusion the family was knit closely one to the other; and Marx is known as having been a devoted father. Once he remarked playfully that children should raise their parents — can this be where "progressive education" had its birth?

The publication of the first volume of *Capital* in 1867 was widely recognized as a landmark in the development of socialist theory, and Marx began to reap some repute in England and abroad. The death of Engels' father permitted the son to provide more generously for his friend; and the Marxes took decent lodgings at last. There he worked at his book, rising at seven for black coffee, working until two in the afternoon, pausing for a brief meal, working again in his study until supper. This was the family hour — what remained of his family, that is — and then Marx was back to work until two or three in the morning.

How Marx organized the First International, a federation of revolutionary thinkers, and scuttled it finally when he seemed to lose control; how he acquired a reputation for having a finger in dark plots on the Continent, which occasionally provoked representations to the British Government; how he brooked no opposition and ruthlessly went his dedicated way — all these things have been written and rewritten, and the reader can find the full story in many items of our Chapter Seven and bibliography. Be it only noted that Jenny, faithful in all things, died in 1882, Marx in 1883, and Engels in 1895.

Was it the end, or the beginning? For Marx the end of a long agony of living out a life of poverty and pain; for the world the beginning of a long agony of living out ideas which would not die.

Looking back over this brief biography, one detects a simple lesson: this man asked nothing of life that he was not prepared to give; he lived convictions at the cost of pride, fame, wealth, power, family — all very dear to him; he *was* before he *wrote*, and he asked no sacrifice of others that he was unwilling to make himself. Is not the lesson obvious: he and his views will not be driven from the stage of history by any lesser dedication and sacrifice! Is this why they have triumphed so often? We do not labor from seven one morning until two or three the next?! We like a little vacation, for all that?! There are minimal comforts, to say no more, we cannot do without?! After all, one must eat, and play, and willingly "sacrifice" (a part of what he does not need) —is it not so?!!

"A spectre is haunting Europe — the spectre of Communism," wrote Marx and Engels as the first sentence of the *Communist Manifesto*. Haunting indeed, and not Europe alone! But has our philosophy of eat, drink, make merry, work a little, play a little, give a little — has it wit enough even to know when it is haunted? and why it is so afraid?

If a genius exacts of those who come after him the obligation to understand him, as Goethe said, a singularly dedicated man exacts of those who defy him an equal dedication. The march of Communism demonstrates this all too well. And there was, too, always his Jenny — as, incidentally, there was Lenin's Krupskaya, and Trotsky's Natalia. The challenge is not to men alone! All this is why Marx has been hated, scorned, derided, but never laughed at. Karl Marx was a gauntlet cast before the world. God so used him, and so uses him still.

MARXISM

What did he accomplish, then, with all his work and poring over bleak and ponderous tomes? Engels sought to sum it up on several occasions. In his *Anti-Duhring*, written in 1877, Engels put it thus: "The materialist conception of history starts from the principle that production, and with production the exchange of its products, is the basis of every social order; that in every society which has appeared in history the distribution of products, and with it the division of society into classes or estates, is determined by what is produced and how it is produced, and how the product is exchanged. According to this conception, the ultimate causes of all social changes and political revolutions are to be sought, not in the minds of men, in their increasing insight into eternal truth and justice, but in changes in the mode of production and exchange; they are to be sought not in the *philosophy* but in the *economics* of the epoch concerned."

In 1888, writing a preface to a new edition of the *Manifesto,* Engels put it thus: " The *Manifesto* being our joint production, I consider myself bound to state that the fundamental proposition which forms its nucleus belongs to Marx. That proposition is: That in every historical epoch, the prevailing mode of economic production and exchange, and the social organization necessarily following from it, form the basis upon which is built up, and from which alone can be explained, the political and intellectual history of that epoch; that consequently the whole history of mankind (since the dissolution of primitive tribal society, holding all land in common ownership) has been a history of class struggles, contests between exploiting and exploited, ruling and oppressed classes; that the history of these class struggles forms a series of evolutions in which, nowadays, a stage has been reached where the exploited and oppressed class—the proletariat — cannot attain its emancipation from the sway of the exploiting and ruling class — the bourgeoisie — without at the same time, and once and for all, emancipating society at large from all exploitation, oppression, class distinctions and class struggles."

If, after the disciple, we wish to hear the master himself, Marx said, in one of his letters, "I was led to the conclusion that legal relations, as well as forms of state, could neither be understood by themselves, nor explained by the so-called general progress of the human mind, but that they are rooted in the material conditions of life which Hegel calls . . . civil society. The anatomy of civil society is to be sought in political economy."

As a thumbnail sketch, Marx's last sentence says it all: "The anatomy of civil society is to be sought in political economy."

But what is this he is saying? The simplest way to make it clear, if, as I suppose, these relatively abstract statements do not explain themselves, is as a beginning to translate what Engels and Marx have been saying into an illustration. Let us make it a "playlet," or melodrama.

The setting is mid-nineteenth century England as Marx knew it, and as Engels has exposed it in his careful study of *The Condition of the Working Class in England,* published in German in 1845, and in English in 1892. The British Government had from time to time concerned itself with these same "conditions" and the reports of Royal Commissions were on file in the British Museum. Marx carefully dug them out.

The scene Marx and Engels viewed was not idyllic. With the Industrial Revolution in full stride, the unrestrained scramble for power and profit — according to the dictates of Adam Smith — exacted a heavy toll in life, limb, spirit, and soul of the men, women, and children who fed the maw of the machine: a working day for men, women, and children alike which commonly began before dawn and extended past sunset, six days a week; working lives begun at six years of age and ended in appalling mortality; children chained to the machines, and beaten to their tasks; accident and disease run rampant, with little or no protection or concern for the victims; immeasurable suffering, grinding poverty, hardship without hope. While Browning might laud Pippa's one holiday in a year, the whole inhuman aspect of early industrialism roused Marx and Engels to bitter condemnation.

It is important, as we move step by step through Marxism, to keep well in mind that background for Marx's thinking. If the description which follows is not, happily, in accord with what we know of American industrial life, let us rejoice that the difference is a measure of the progress capitalism, under state supervision, has made in self-correction. The significance of this self-correction remains for later discussion. It was not only a refutation of Marx, but also one of Adam Smith.

Keeping this background in mind, then, and reckoning with the recalcitrance which all illustrations tend to exhibit, take the following playlet as an introduction to the meaning of the paragraphs quoted from Marx and Engels above.

"We Make Tea Tables"

The Scene: a small factory, where are made Ye Tip-Topple Tea Tables.

The Place: anywhere in not-so-merrie olde Englande.

The Time: mid-nineteenth century, or so.

The Characters: eleven of us, divided as follows:

You: one of ten employees.

Me: the boss and owner of the place.

PROLETARIAT AND BOURGEOISIE

First Note: The division of the cast displays two basic terms with which all playgoers must become thoroughly familiar. The ten employees belong to the class which Marx has immortalized by the name *proletariat.* This term comprehends all those persons who have no economic resources between themselves and starvation except what they obtain, almost day to day, from the sale of their *labor power,* which they must sell in order to keep alive and to feed their families. Inasmuch as labor power is really a part of the man himself, the proletariat are those who sell, or alienate, *themselves* for so many hours a day in order to live — and thus to sell more of themselves. Marx calls it wage slavery. But *proletariat* is not only an opprobrius term. It became also a fighting word, calling the masses to revolution. And it is from this class that Marx expects salvation by way of revolt to come; the proletariat is the "suffering savior" of Marxist "theology."

It is further to be noted that another class is defined by the cast of our playlet. The owner of the factory belongs to the *bourgeoisie,* those who *own the means of production.* This class has resources enough to live, if need be, without being forced to sell their labor power, though some of them may in fact work harder and longer than do some of the proletariat. It is not a difference in effort expended which distinguishes the bourgeoisie from the proletariat, nor a difference in kind of work, though the connotation of the terms in Marxist usage is that the hardships and the hard labor generally fall on the proletariat's shoulders, while ease, luxury and indolence are more commonly the lot of the bourgeoisie. The real difference between the two classes arises out of the *ownership* of the means of production, which resides in the hands of the bourgeoisie. From this basic difference all others flow, as we shall soon see. Let us to the playlet.

Act One:

The factory, at close of day. Amidst small talk, the workmen gather and prepare for shipment eleven tea tables — the product this day, as every day, of our work. There are, the perceptive playgoer will notice at once (and this the players must make clear to the not-so-perceptive) *eleven* tea tables — that is, *one* for *each* employee plus one for the employer. (There are certain statistical and pedagogical advantages in this coincidence.)

A van lumbers up, the horses champing at their bits, already late for hay and rest. The tea tables are carefully conveyed to the van, and the audience is given to understand that they are now en route to market.

Wearily, ten of the players don their greatcoats (for it is winter) and leave the stage. Silence descends upon the establishment, except for the audible figuring aloud of the plant owner, as he chews still further the stub of his pencil between covering his ledger with illegible symbols. He has a problem.

The Theory of Labor Value

Note Two: (We may at any point, when the depth of his struggles has been made indubitably clear to the audience, allow the plant owner to pull the curtain on Act One. It is, in fact, quite over, and has served well. Do you remember the two *classes?* Marx never forgot them. Do you recall how many tea tables? and how many workmen? and how many — excuse me — who was the owner? Then, down with the curtain, while the mystery of the plant owner's figuring is explained.)

These tea tables puzzle the owner. It is as simple as that. He wants to be just — to his employees and to himself — and to pay them (and himself) for the *real value* of their work. But he is stuck on what *value* really is. And if he cannot arrive at that, then he is likely to fall back upon the useful theory of learned and successful economist David Ricardo, that his wages shall always be paid only to the measure necessary to enable workmen to reproduce young workmen — and that not in uncommon style or luxury. After all, Parson Malthus had proved persuasively enough that the poor simply overbegot when overpaid, and this led always to starvation. No call to encourage *that!*

Yet to be fair — what, then, is *value?* Zip up the curtain, and let us have:

Act Two:

Same setting, same puzzled owner with pencil now devoured. Enter a ghost, wearing black beard, clearly labeled by placard on his back: Karl Marx.

Ho, ho, says our ghost, waving his delicate and expressive hands, so you are perplexed? Be perplexed no longer, though you will not care overly much for what I have to say!

First, one must distinguish between *value* and *price*. Price is what is actually paid in current coin for those tea tables on the market; it may or may not approximate their real value. *Real value* cannot be measured in terms of use, desire, demand, marginal utility, or even need. All of these factors influence *price* but are external to the tea tables themselves and hence cannot touch or modify *value*. Ideally, of course, *price* and *value* meet, but this, my friend (and the ghost shakes a ghostly finger under plant owner's nose), can only be guaranteed by the communized society!

But what is the *real value,* then? (I — the plant owner — say meekly.)

It is, says the ghost, the amount of "socially necessary labor" which goes into making the tables. What went to market in that van, therefore, is *labor power,* which has conferred upon the raw materials which go into tea tables all the real value the tables possess. Raw materials, likewise, are wealth, it is true, but have *real value* only in so far as labor power went into foresting, mining, raising, or otherwise obtaining them. Labor creates value. Nothing else can! Moreover, not all labor creates *real* value, as the amount of labor wasted upon some of your foolish pleasures (again that finger) amply shows! Labor expended upon those things *society needs,* my friend, that is the only kind of labor which creates *real* value! And, shall I note in passing, the only way to make sure that this kind of "socially necessary" labor is all the labor expended in merrie olde Englande is by rigid state control. You do not like this I see. Didn't think you would. Happily the era subjugated to your likes and dislikes will not last forever.

Note Three: It is a matter of indifference at this point whether the curtain remains drawn to show ghost and owner in vigorous disputation, or falls to the sound of muffled epithets and violent struggle. We have made our point, to be summarized here only for those who dozed a little during the ghost's solo part: Marx has expounded his famous *theory of labor value.* It was not his exactly, and he did not hesitate to attribute it to, of all people, Benjamin Franklin, as well as to David Ricardo. It may be traced back, if one has a nose for such adventures, through Adam Smith and John Locke into medieval thinkers. No doubt one could, as some scholars always do, find it adumbrated by the Greeks. The audience will simply remember that *only labor* — manual and mental — creates value; and, what is more specifically Marx's contribution to the theory, only *socially necessary* labor creates *real value.* The fact that under capitalism the employment of labor is spent upon luxuries long before all necessities have been met, means for Marx that capitalism is not the best form for the selective use of a nation's labor force.

There could be, at this point, an Intermission. Perhaps the stage director, peeking discreetly underneath the curtain, can ascertain if one is necessary to keep the audience alert. Sooner or later, in any event, we come again to:

THE THEORY OF SURPLUS VALUE

Act Three

Same place next morning. This is pay day. Why that should take place first thing in the morning is not evident, except that this strategem eliminates the necessity of having eleven tea tables standing around waiting for that moving van. Moreover, for the dialectical exercises awaiting the workmen on this memorable day, they must needs be fresh and alert with a will for any fate. That state of mind is best achieved in the new light of day.

It must appear that the workmen, too, have been thinking. They did not do this in consort, nor did they meet together. The law prohibits workmen from meeting off-hours together, even for a cup of tea, the better to prevent them from arriv-

ing at just such conclusions as they have (in our play) simul-
taneously (and, as it were, quite miraculously) thought of
just before the curtain rose this fine bleak morning.

If the law did not forbid it, we would give them one
spokesman; but since that would risk him the gallows, and
we do not want to introduce the police until later for another purpose, it is best that the following declarations be
spread somewhat evenly abroad among all ten. The astute
director will manage this. Perhaps each can speak one word
consecutively, or occasionally they can mouth a phrase in
unison. The play, after all, is *the thing;* small matter how
you go about it. To get on, then, if the Intermission is over
— or if there has been none: Up curtain!

The workmen are mumbling to themselves and to each
other. This can be done under the law if the mumbling
does not sound conspiratorial. Not having seen the ghost,
nor heard of him, they have some margin of safety.

It is obvious at once to the sensitive member of the
audience that employer and employee have been running,
in their thoughts, in one channel — no evidence at all of
greatness of mind, in this case. It is the channel, not to say
rut, of wages. The workmen have an idea; not an idea
sophisticated enough to comprehend the intricacies of Price
and Value (after all, they missed the ghost!) but definite
for their purposes. All this must now come out, as before
directed, in dialogue which does not display conspiracy or
previous consultation; it would be a poor ending — even
for this play — to have half the labor force swinging from the
gallows in the cold morning light. Though, thoughtfully,
Parson Malthus, mentor Ricardo, and even Professor Smith
provided for this contingency, too — not quite alone,
to be sure, but with some assists from the great estate holders
who had driven people out of their homes and into the
slums of the cities by "enclosing" the land. These "en-
closures" made sheep meadows out of small farms and
villages, leaving the small farmers and the villagers who,
alas, grew no wool on their backs, to shift as best they might
for themselves. Wool paid well; small farmers and villagers
paid less well. Therefore — did you guess? — *enclose* the
land! Business is business, and sentiment earns no interest!

By this nicety, and by the authority of Malthus, *et al.,*
the supply of workers to take the place of those hanged for

conspiracy, or for theft of a loaf of bread, or other equally monstrous infringements of the law was always sufficient to replace the loss. This fact, which got noised around soon enough, discouraged conspiracy, which is loose talk in a crowd of three or four; and, except when a father could no longer endure seeing his children starve, tended to keep thievery at a minimum. If the starving knew that even St. Thomas Aquinas had sanctioned "theft" of necessities by those who would otherwise starve, they seldom acted upon the knowledge. The law knew nothing of it; and Aquinas was both long dead and, on this score, more or less officially forgotten by the priests and prelates who represented him in the world.

But, such digression! while the audience waits more or less breathlessly, for *Act Three*. The mumbling on stage cannot go on forever. Out with it! What *Idea* did you ten proletarians have?

It turns out that the *idea* is simple, too simple to cope with price and value theory. It rests upon an already established fact: we *eleven* actors (me, too) make *eleven* tea tables. (Remember?) Why not, the workmen want to know, take *all* the money received for these tables, deduct from it the necessary expenses for materials and plant operation, and then *divide* it into eleven parts — *one* part for each table, and — see how neatly this has been planned — *one equal share* for each of us, eleven, including the owner. Share and share alike! What could be more fair?

At the conclusion of this somewhat disjointed (the words, you remember, are parcelled out a little) statement of economic theory, the workmen applaud themselves for their wisdom, and stop short when they observe that I, the employer, stand with hands conspicuously folded over my chest. Something, they detect, is amiss. I fill them in.

Haven't they forgotten a little, significant matter? (There can be majesty in the tone and stance — if the right actor is selected for the part.) All eyes are glued on my folded arms. I slowly extend one of them, sweep it in a practiced circle about the factory, and say, in sufficiently sepulchral tones: *Who owns* all that you behold here? (At this the audience feels the thrill of the climax of the play; the workmen shudder and dare not contradict my obvious intent by casting so much as a glance at *their* coats hanging from pegs on

the wall — all but these, alas, I do indeed own. And were it
not for my munificence ... men have gone without coats
before and survived. Eh? Had they been paid too much?
Wasting money on coats — in the dead of winter? They slink
to their benches. The making of tea tables commences. No
murmuring is heard. The manager takes out a new pencil
and commences to devour it, bit by bit.)

The Act is over. For those bewildered by the strange
force so simple a statement of ownership exerted over incipi-
ent rebellion, we move to:

Note Four: You have now been inducted, or conducted, into
the sanctuary of Marxism. The fearsome power my words exercised upon the workmen resides in the key term of Marxist
"econology": *surplus value!*

Capital, said Marx when he was very much not a ghost, *does
not labor!* It only makes labor possible, under capitalism, by
providing what is congealed labor in the form of buildings,
machines, and so on. *Capital creates no value!*

Exchange, no matter how involved, *does not create value
either,* and so the market cannot give real value to anything.
(These views might be traced back to Aristotle by the assiduous.
Marx took what he needed where he found it. Aristotle had said
that money is sterile, and the Church of the Middle Ages concluded from this principle that interest, called *usury,* was therefore prohibited. Marx knew this, of course, but he was not given
to seeking authority for his views in teachings of the Church. He
simply asserted that neither capital, nor exchange, nor any other
relationship could create value—of course not, for he had already
affirmed that *only* labor, socially necessary labor at that, can
create value. That some labor goes into exchange Marx tended
to ignore.)

To make a long argument short, and not to keep the audience
waiting too long for the Last Act — it cometh — my ownership of
the factory entitles me, I think, to a *profit. One eleventh* of the
total income may be my "share" but whence then my *profit?* The
justice of this query is what silenced the workmen at once, even
though it was unexpressed.

Well, where will it come from, this profit to which I am
entitled? Only from labor, for only from labor comes *any* value.

Whose labor? You workmen now tremble on the threshold of
understanding that truth which cowed you at once. *My* profit

comes out of *your labor*. From the value which you create and invest in tea tables I skim off a *surplus* which I take as my own — as profit on my investment in plant and machines. I take from you *surplus value,* the key to Marxist economic theory, though the idea was developed by Ricardo.

The audience now understands the ways of the world in the maze of economics. Labor, which is all the proletariat has to sell, creates value — this is *the theory of labor value*. Profit, which is the motive force of capitalism, arises only out of *surplus value,* that is out of paying the workman for *less* value than his labor creates.

Note: There is another, and Last Act, in store; but one or two matters must be made clear first. Perhaps the stage manager can invite some professor of economics to desert his ivory tower long enough to lecture the audience about these while the actors take an earned rest. But professors are notoriously reluctant to mix with the crowd, and to get his players a breather the stage manager may have to do the lecture himself. For such an emergency, here is the text:

THE FAIR WAGE

First, point out that Marx spent a lot of time on this matter of wages. What is a "fair" wage? And how can it be *scientifically* determined? If surplus value was not the answer, what was? Marx began by supposing that the amount of socially necessary labor which went into goods, and as an afterthought, services, could somehow be measured — and then paid for. He gave this up, as has everyone but the Technocrats of yesteryear, and finally settled for a slogan: from each according to his ability, and to each according to his need. (He did not suppose that this measure would be taken seriously before startling changes had been made in the economic structure of society.) Oddly enough — you may wish to point out — this slogan is rather close to a statement of the views of John Calvin on the same subject. (No record exists of Marx's devotion to Calvin, however.)

Second, show that Marx carefully studied the ways in which wages *were actually determined* in the industries of his time, and thus came upon another formula which he borrowed from classical economics and turned to his own account. The workmen were, Marx saw, only *commodities* themselves, for sale or barter on the open market. Wages were, in effect, the *market price* for these living commodities. Men and things were bought for a price, indifferently and with no special consideration for the difference between the human and the material. Because of competition for these human commodities, the supply of which often exceeded the demand, their market price — that is, their wage — was beaten down to a minimum. And what was that minimum? The audience already knows: the cost of subsistence for the workmen, plus the cost of reproduction of his kind to insure a next generation of workmen. That is all. That sentiment or religious indignation must not influence this freely determined market price of the commodity of labor had long since been demonstrated by that economic trinity: Malthus, Ricardo, and Smith. Ricardo had even given the process a name: *the iron law of wages*. Would even a Bishop tamper with an iron law? It is not recorded that for some time any Bishop did.

Third, and last (this is still a text for the stage manager, who, in default of a disciple of Ricardo or Smith, carries on in the best tradition of the playhouse ... while behind the scenes the actors relax for tribulations yet to come), give the audience to understand that Marx found, then, that *wages* and *surplus value* were in fact related like this: after the workmen have worked just long enough into the day to produce a value equal to the wages they receive, the rest of their day's labor goes into surplus value. The ratio between these two parts of the day is fixed by the price paid for finished goods, on the one hand, and the price paid in overhead and wages, on the other. This ratio tended to vary, and the temptation to make it vary in his favor kept the employer on the lookout for higher prices, cheaper labor, more work per hour, less investment in plant, equipment, and safety devices. This is what the Royal Reports demonstrated, and what Engels had discovered for himself.

Final Word: for those members of the audience whose sympathies have not been won by the workmen, and who feel that the employer has, after all, a right to some profit on his investment, you may point out that Marx was well aware of such sentiments. He simply asked some difficult questions, with which you may beguile the audience briefly: Marx viewed all the means of production, the factories and machines and railroads as *congealed labor*. If, he inquired, you as *owner* of these things did not make them yourself, then *whose* labor are you *claiming* as your own, and how did you get to thinking you had such a claim? Either you have been taking surplus value for some time now, or you have inherited it from someone who did.

The long, if not anxiously, awaited Last Act is about to begin.
The manager retires, mopping his brow; the players go back to
their benches. The curtain, thin wall between two worlds, rises.
It is, the audience is given to know, almost time for noon lunch.
Unless this factory is uncommon, lunch is eaten while work
goes on; but for purposes of the play (wonderful make-believe
world where the impossible is almost possible) we will ring a
gong to announce the hour of noon and allow the workmen
to gather together for bread and cold water — not for long, of
course. How shall we get eleven tables made, if . . . .

CLASS STRUGGLE

Act the Last:

Workmen sitting on saw-horses and floor, eating. They
mumble together. One rises and walks out; then another,
and a third. At last only five are left. The manager is off-
stage and does not notice this diminution of his labor force.
Then he comes on, and, to stress the fact to the unwary that
five players *have* left the stage, he shouts: *What goes on
here?!* (A certain imprecision in verb tense must be allowed
him, under the stress of the moment; he should, of course,
have asked: What *has gone* on here, as any purist would
willingly have missed the point just to tell him—)

This stentorian cry, issued as it is by his omnipotence,
The Boss, brings the remaining five workmen to their feet,
and shocks one of them into utterance. He steps forward.
His now-or-never, do-or-die air electrifies the audience. Can
this be a workman, England, in the year of Victoria . . . !
(Well, no, it isn't; it is only on the stage, and we still are
not ready for those policemen apromised aforetime — be
patient, they will come when necessary. So let the workman
find his tongue.)

What does he say in this brief moment of glory? He says
that you workmen are tired of surplus value! That, at least,
is what he means. His words are to the effect that they want
higher wages, here and now!

The employer, taken aback for a moment, quickly regains
his aplomb.

Oh, indeed? Well, well! Have they considered the consequences of this rash demand? To his surprise they have. It
turns out, as the exchange grows more heated, that this is

precisely *why* five of the workmen are missing! Either they
get a raise or ... well, why not out with it: the five are out
scouting up better jobs, places to work where (they mean
to say) surplus value is *not* taken from their backs.

The employer laughs ... not a nice sound at all, a grat-
ing, dismal, cackling sound which fills the theater and pre-
pares the audience for what now occurs. A sound is heard
at the factory door. It opens. A man slinks in. It is workman number six. He need not be asked. He got no new job!
His hand trembles as he hangs his coat back on the peg.
Wordless he goes to his bench, his lunch bulging from his
coat pocket, untouched. He starts work. The other five
workmen drop back, their spokesman once more losing his
voice. The employer's laughter grows no more dulcet in tone
as one by one the other four workmen, striving to make
themselves invisible, steal in, hang up coats, and creep back
to work.

The audience does not have to be told in words: they
know. Either the workman accepts surplus value as a fixture
in the firmament of his narrow life, or he can choose to
starve, and all his family with him. Something pathetic
about this creeping, crawling, beaten humanity touches
audience and employer alike. The laughter ceases; and the
pencil comes out again. With audible sigh the audience
awaits the curtain.

But it does not fall. (We now await the policeman!) A
taste of freedom has been too much for that one workman
who acted as unchosen spokesman for the rest. Throwing
down his hammer he strides once again to the center of the
stage. The others, aghast, watch him, stark terror written on
their faces. He stops before the pencil-chewer. He finds his
voice again, at last, and in cracked tone shouts: There are
ten of us, and only one of you! We are stronger, any one of
us, than you! Why not throw you out, then, and run the
factory ourselves? Trembling with his own insecurity the
man reaches for the employer. The others rise from their
benches and converge upon the pair.

And then the door opens and a policeman enters! He is
the neighbor of the workman who has found his long-lost
voice; his children play in the muddy lanes with the workman's infant. Help us, shouts the workman, and receives a
sharp blow upon the head from the officer's stick, and then

another and a third. As he falls to his knees, and the others return hastily to their work, the audience understands how the police power of the state protects the taking of surplus value; and behind the policeman, not well hidden, stands the hangman.

Shall we drop the curtain now, or shall we watch as the spokesman who has for the last time lost his voice is dragged off to a certain engagement with that hangman? Shall we allow the audience to go home, or shall we allow the employer to remove from his lips the chewed pencil and to lecture to his little cowed flock on the economic facts of life?

Listen to him, if you like, as he summarizes for us what the playlet has meant to teach — that is, Marx's meaning, and Engels', in the quotations we have read:

Let us (he says, striding to the center of the stage with a pardonable swagger) recapitulate briefly the little lessons learned lately about Marxism.

We have seen vividly portrayed the meaning of *bourgeoisie,* of *proletariat,* of *labor value,* of *surplus value.* Knowing the meaning of these, we grasp the thrust of Marx's economic theories. We see how the state is shaped by economic relations. Of all this you ten workmen were ignorant at first. (At some point in the following pages, quietly, slowly, the curtain will descend, and real life will merge with the make-believe of the stage. We employ this device to suggest that in so far as the playlet was true to Marx, it *was real life,* as Marx saw it, the most real that life can be.)

(We let the employer speak on, now . . .)

When you caught on to what was happening, you did not rejoice in it. (Helping you "catch on" is what the Marxist means by "patiently explain.")

So, you complain, perhaps, and I (perhaps) am understanding. "Go work elsewhere," I say sweetly; and off you go. But you soon make a startling discovery: all industry in capitalism takes its profit in surplus value. On Marxist grounds, profit can come from nowhere else. You now face a relatively simple, and permanent, choice: work for the bourgeoisie, and lose surplus value, or, if you prefer, starve! The word *proletariat* takes on grim significance now. You begin to see why it forms one of the revolutionary springs of Marxism. You have nothing between you and death except your labor power, which you must sell to the highest bidder no matter what he bids, or you die, and your family with you!

You have learned in the best way what Marx might have called an elementary lesson in social philosophy: economic relations, that is, having a job and how much you are paid for it, prices and rents and hours of labor — all of these relations are the most basic in life. Indeed, they govern life ... and death! This is what Marx means in common terms, when he says that economic relations govern all the rest of life. Men are slaves of things, and even the bourgeoisie, if they wished to, could not escape their economic position.

When you become aware of these facts of economic life, you ten workmen sense a common ground which you share against me. You consciously form one *class*. I sense the same thing, and however much I may be in competition with other bourgeoisie, I consciously form another *class* with them. These two classes stand opposed, divided forever (until the revolution) by the fact of surplus value. Between them there arises endless struggle, the proletariat seeking to survive and to improve its position, and the bourgeoisie seeking to enslave them further. This is the Marxist doctrine of *class struggle,* another burning phrase in Communist propaganda. It accounts for the scorn the Marxist feels for the member of the proletariat who deliberately tries to defend or support the bourgeoisie. To make *all* members of the proletariat *class conscious* is one of the tasks of Communist propaganda.

Economic Determinism

Engels writes that the class struggle accounts for the organization of society, and the changes which make history. How do economic relations *determine* the social structure of any society in any epoch?

Let us begin with the institution of widest influence, the state. By *state* I mean the whole apparatus of political organization, including the executive power, the legislature, the bureaus, the courts, the military and the police power. All these *determined* in form and conduct by economics? Yes, said Marx, in their broad outlines precisely so!

Returning to the tea table factory, let us illustrate what Marx means. You ten workmen decided to take my factory away from me, and to run it yourselves in order to keep the full value of your own labor.

Ten of you against one of me. It should have been simple. But what happens when you try to evict me? I call the police. They look like men who might be your neighbors, but they don't take your side; they take mine. Behind them stand the militia and the army. They also, if necessary, take my side. So does the judge, and the law. Behind the judge stand the prisons . . . and the gallows. Even they are on my side. You learn, thus, that much of the state apparatus is formed and operated, Marx says, just to protect the right of the bourgeoisie to take surplus value from the proletariat. Economic relations "create" the nature of the state.

If you decide to meet at someone's house to discuss, say, a strike against me, you will find that parliament has thoughtfully passed a decree against "unlawful assembly." Parliament acts in conformity to the economic situation.

If I invest my money abroad, the state employs the army and navy to protect my taking surplus value from strange peoples, keeps trade routes open, and insures my access to raw materials. In short, the whole field of international relations and international law takes shape and substance from economic relations.

Not the state only, but all institutions are shaped by economic relations, the Marxist insists. Let us take but two others.

Consider education. Your children (if they are lucky in this *nineteenth* century) go to school. They learn the three R's. They also learn cheerfully to accept things as they are, to obey the laws, to measure a man's greatness by how much of surplus value he has accumulated (called *success*) for himself, to recognize that the greatest men in the community are those who most rapidly acquire the largest measure of possessions. The whole atmosphere of education arises from the economic situation, to say nothing of the textbooks and teacher appointments.

At the universities, too, whole departments of economic theory exist to justify the status quo, and to furnish teachers who believe in it. Was it not Adam Smith, learned professor of moral philosophy, who demonstrated that an enlightened self-interest always works for the greatest good of all? Did he not thus *prove* that by getting the most for ourselves we bourgeoisie benefit everyone, even the proletariat? And what of that amiable cleric, Thomas R. Malthus, who taught the lesson university economics departments elaborate, that a population always outgrows its food supply, and therefore starvation is both natural and necessary — among certain classes, of course. From which did not

David Ricardo demonstrate that if I raise my wages, by an iron law of nature you incontinent workmen will simply engender larger families until someone starves just the same? Higher education, too, is formed by economic realities, as might be shown concerning all the other university departments, Marx argues.

Take one more social institution, the church. Marx called religion the opium of the people. Like opium it dulled their sense of pain at their exploitation. Let the pastor or the priest promise you eternal bliss in exchange for patient acceptance of your present condition. Let the church teach you to obey the laws, to respect property and position, to refrain from violence, to accept your lot as ordained by heaven itself. Let the church fortify its admonitions with lively pictures of eternal disaster for those who disobey. Religion becomes thus a valuable element in the class struggle. We of the bourgeoisie support it gladly enough in exchange for its temporal benefits. Of course, we cannot allow it to interfere with the laws of the market. Religion, too, Marx informs us, takes its form and character from the economic situation.

This kind of inferential study of all institutions and customs which prevail in any epoch, tracing the character of each back to the economic relations which cause it, is what the Marxist has in mind when he says that no epoch or civilization can be understood apart from an understanding of the relations of production and exchange which occur in it.

If it were true that economic relations condition all other human relations, then changes in human relations would be but the *reflection* of changes in economic relations. This is exactly what Marx maintains. It is the basis of his philosophy of history.

A philosophy of history is an attempt to explain why things change. Why, we might ask, is life today so different from life in the Middle Ages? Marx's answer is that the relations of production and exchange are different from what they were in the Middle Ages, and all other differences follow upon these.

He distinguishes four periods in human history, each characterized by the forms of production and exchange which supported it, and each becoming the next when those forms changed.

The first was that of the nomadic tribes. *Because* all productive enterprise, principally the herds and the grazing lands, was held in common within the tribe, there was brotherhood, and peace and mutual respect and security in tribal social life. *Because* the separate tribes did not hold productive goods in common, there arose wars between them. These led to the taking of prisoners as slaves.

The second period of human history arose when slaves began to perform economic functions. A wholly different civilization now began, the toiling many carrying on their backs the leisured few; and what men have been pleased to call culture flourished parasitically. As wars weakened the powerful conquerors, one after the other, economic relations changed, even as they caused the wars. Gradually economic functions came to be performed by semi-freemen, who sold their allegiance to powerful lords in exchange for land and protection. On the back of this new series of relationships in production and exchange, the feudal ages were erected.

This third period derived its peculiar characteristics from the agricultural, barter, handicraft economy which underlay it. And then as the guilds arose, the trades flourished, the third estate came to commercial power, and the cities grew. The economic basis of feudalism changed to that of the modern world.

The fourth period of history was born. Now, as Engels notes, this period is the last in which exploitation and class struggle will endure. The capitalism which arose out of feudalism and the Middle Ages so sharply distinguishes those who own the means of production from those who do not, that class consciousness can be clear and precise, and the final revolution to destroy all private ownership in the means of production can be achieved.

Then will come the fifth and final period of human history, which will be discussed shortly.

This is Marx's sketch of the course of history. The changes recorded in customs, beliefs, institutions and ways of life all do but reflect the basic changes which occurred in economic relations.

Description, of course, is not explanation. Even if history did follow the course Marx described, the question still remains: what *causes* economic change? Marx's answer is (according to some of his followers) his most significant contribution to intellectual history.

DIALECTICAL MATERIALISM

Marx borrowed the *form* of his answer from the German philosopher Hegel, who is the father of modern philosophy of history. It is called the *dialectic,* which comes from a Greek word meaning *to argue*. This meaning is not a bad expression of Marx and Hegel's use of the term. How Marx made this idea the clue to the understanding of economic change, and therefore the clue to all historical change, may be illustrated by returning once again to our tea table factory.

You will remember that I, as owner, invested my capital in that factory for only one reason: to make a profit. This is the nature of capital investment: it is made only in order to obtain a profit. In order to make that profit, I *had* to employ workmen. So I hired you ten workmen to join me in making tea tables ... *for profit*. Now, notice carefully, and the word dialectic will take on concrete significance. *In order to get the profit for which alone I made my investment, I had to take surplus value from you.* But my doing so *made* you my *class enemy*. My investment, for profit, *called into being* a class which became my deadly enemy. Or, in other words, capital always creates its own "contra- diction." This is what Marx means by *dialectic*. Not only is this true of capitalism, but it is true of every society in which the means of production have been in the hands of private owners. The owners always *create* the class which opposes them.

Between the owning class and the exploited class there is always tension, struggle, and release of energy. It is this struggle which gradually brings about (more accurately, *reflects,* but see page 86ff.) change in economic relations. Upon these changes in economic relations, caused by the energy released by class struggle, all other historical changes rest.

Marx now has his answer to the question of *why* history changes, that is, more accurately, why history is *history*. This answer is called *dialectical materialism,* that is, matter arguing with itself causes historical progress. These two polysyllables are a formidable verbal whip in the hands of the Marxist, but they are simply a shorthand for one explanation of history among many.

The word *materialism* in Marx's theory of history means that it is changes among material forces, coming to social ex- pression in economic relations, which guide the course of history and provide the energy which motivates it. The word *dialectical* means that the forces of history act in self-developed opposition to each other in producing movement.

Readers of Marx are tempted to raise the moral question: are the bourgeoisie, then, so desperately bad? To ask the question is to reveal a misapprehension of what Marx has taught concerning historical forces. The kind of man the capitalist is, or the kind of men the feudal lords and ancient slave-holders were, really alters nothing in the relationship between exploiters and exploited. Men are the pawns of economic forces, not their masters. Capital, for example, is by definition investment for profit. Under a capitalist system some will own the capital, some will not; both are caught in the web of relationships capitalism creates. Should, say, one plant owner, moved by compassion, raise his wages without concern for the market, the laws of capitalist exchange would in time rob him of his business. When Robert Owen, the British businessman-philanthropist, tried to get other mill owners to imitate the example he set in humane treatment of labor at New Lanark, his argument had to be that labor, so treated, produced more goods. This was not because Owen did not himself act upon other motives, but because the extent of "humanity" he could show was relative to the rate at which goods continued to be produced at his mills.

Economic relations based upon the private ownership of the means of production establish inexorable roles for both bourgeoisie and proletariat. They do not make them; they only play them. The stage upon which the drama is enacted is not dependent upon human will; the script controls the players and limits the scope of their activity. If one man is squeamish about it, others will take his place. The play goes on until the very stage itself is changed, that is, until basic economic relationships dialectically modify themselves.

Why does the dialectic apply to economic relations? Could there be any of these not governed by dialectic? No, *not* so long as there is *private* ownership of the means of production. So long as men, any men, can take legal title to the productive means, the class struggle is inevitable. And out of this struggle come all those personal and social evils which darken life for both proletariat and bourgeoisie, though in different ways for each. This struggle perverts the very nature of man, arouses the worst in him, and turns the fruits of his labors into ashes. It is every man for himself — and many there be who are hindmost; even some who seem to be first.

This is why, then, the Marxists sneer at any program which aims at less than the complete overthrow of private property in the means of production. "Dreamers" and "Utopians," who hindered the coming of the revolution, they called all who wished by legislative means or moral suasion to soften the edges of the class struggle.

REVOLUTION, DICTATORSHIP, PARADISE

We can move on now to the last element in Marxism. What will be the answer to social evil? The answer will be the violent revolt against the established order, by the proletariat, led by intellectuals who have deserted the ranks of the bourgeoisie as they have come to see the real misery of the proletariat, and the true cause of it. Only after private ownership of the productive means is destroyed can social salvation be achieved.

Obviously the bourgeoisie will take less than kindly to this violent expropriation. When we reflect that Marx maintains that behind the bourgeoisie stands the whole social structure, and all organized force, it is clear that only by heroic and violent action can the revolution be waged successfully.

Heroic action is not easily called into being. It involves sacrifice, danger and death. Even the proletariat must be hard pressed indeed to enter upon so dangerous a way out of their predicament. The great significance of Marxist theory as a revolutionary tool is that it exposes to the proletariat the cause of its exploitation, the one cure, and the true leadership.

Marx maintained that capitalism entailed the "law of the increasing misery of the proletariat." Eventually this misery would make any adventure seem less to endure.

He based this "law" upon an analysis of capitalism as investment for profit. The forces of the market, he reasoned, would drive the bourgeoisie closer and closer together, as they saw more and more clearly that monopoly provides more profit than competition. This expanding concentration of power would be used to exact ever greater profit at the expense of the proletariat, whose position would grow ever relatively more insecure.

Further, more and more of the population would be forced, Marx reasoned, into the ranks of the proletariat. As the small business man sees his enterprise absorbed by mammoth competitors, he becomes a wage earner. The small farmer is driven off his farm by expanding company farming, and joins the ranks of the proletariat. The middle class is gradually wiped out, and finally capitalist society consists of two classes locked in deadly struggle. The antagonism between them is evident to everyone, whether he belong to one or the other, and both classes achieve full class consciousness.

Lenin developed the argument that capitalism cannot, because of investment for profit, pay labor for all it produces. Labor, in turn, cannot purchase enough of the national product to keep the wheels of industry moving. There are crises and depressions. The bourgeoisie turn to foreign markets to sell their excess goods, and in the international competition for foreign territory, the powerful nations come to war among themselves. Thus imperialism leads but to war and intensified suffering for the proletariat.

Marx proposed one other ground for anticipating the revolt of the proletariat. He called it *alienation,* a term and idea borrowed from the German theologian, Ludwig Feuerbach, whose materialism also influenced that of Marx. When a workman makes an object, like a tea table, he gives something of his skill, his mind, his very self to the task. Something of the workman is *in* the object he has made. When, therefore, the owner takes that object as surplus value, he robs the workman of his very *self.* He *alienates* a part of the workman's being. This fact, says Marx, digs deep the gulf between proletariat and bourgeoisie. In the language of philosophy, this is the metaphysical basis of the class struggle: one class robs the other of its very being. Of course, the proletariat does not understand it this way. But that does not change the reality of it, any more than our not seeing the stars in the daylight hours alters the fact that they do shine as brightly then as ever. Alienation is a reality of which the victims are not conscious, but it is at the root of a nascent hatred which can be fanned into revolutionary flame by appeals to more concrete aspects of exploitation. It furnishes the oil which burns in the fierce hatred of more visible injustice.

The growing discontent which Marx envisioned among the proletariat must be focussed, guided and directed to revolutionary ends by the leadership of renegade bourgeois intellectuals. They will select a few of the best fitted among the proletariat for positions of subordinate leadership. They will plan and wait for a "revolutionary situation." When the nation is distressed by the tensions of war or depression, they will strike! The proletariat will be roused to that exertion of power which will bear the old order away by irresistible force. The leaders will be installed as the new centers of authority.

What then? Marx did not speculate too much about the exact nature of what would follow. In a letter written in 1852 Marx says that the class struggle leads inevitably to the "dictatorship of the proletariat," and that this dictatorship leads to "the class-less society."

After managing the first Marxist revolution, Lenin expanded a little on the first step, the dictatorship of the proletariat. A revolution is, after all, a process. It meets with opposition. It has to struggle grimly for victory. This calls for the centralization of authority in the hands of the leadership. Because this authority rests upon the massive power residing in the proletariat, it may be called the dictatorship of the proletariat. It is so called in Russia, even long after it has been used against the proletariat itself.

In theory the dictatorship of the proletariat is a transitional stage by which society enters the fifth period of history. In this transitional stage the leaders take absolute authority into their own hands, as the gift of the proletariat of course, in order to purge society of the last vestige of capitalism and capitalist. No deed is wrong which furthers the ends of the revolution as defined by the leaders, who make their own law. That is why it is futile to argue with a Marxist about the moral crimes committed in Russia. He cuts the ground from under the discussion by pointing out that his critic's morality is "bourgeois," while his is "Communist justice." Under "Communist justice," any deed is right which forwards the revolution, and any deed is wrong which hinders it. No other standards apply.

It must not be supposed that the dictatorship of the proletariat "makes" history. It, like all other social phenomena, *reflects* economic relations. What the dictatorship of the proletariat accomplishes in history is to bring social relations into line with productive relations. Production in the industrial era is, says Marx, social production. A manufactured product is, in reality, a social product, the fruit of the combined effort of many laborers from all over the world. Individualism in production is long dead. If, however, the real relations in production are communal in character, then society will reflect these economic relations. This reflection is accomplished by the dictatorship of the proletariat, which purges society of the individualistic elements left from the capitalist era.

The class which worked the means of production, the proletariat, would come into possession of the means of production. One and the same class would work and would own. The basis for class struggle would be done away. This is what Engels means when he wrote, in our quotation, that the proletariat, when it gains its own emancipation will "at the same time, and once and for all, emancipate society at large from all exploitation, oppression, class distinctions and class struggles."

The state, says Lenin, will "wither away." Why? Because the state is, you recall, but the agent of the exploiting class. With no more exploitation, there will be no more need for the state.

What would become of history itself, which was propelled by the energies released by class struggle? Strictly speaking, it would cease. Time would pass, of course, but the only economic changes to be reflected in society would be those leading to ever greater production, ever more leisure for all, and so history in the present sense would, with the dialectic, be transformed into universal tranquility and peace. The economic law would be, in the words of Marx: "From each according to his ability, and to each according to his need." The millennium would be ushered in, on earth and in time. Evil, which is the fruit of class struggle, would be done away. The development of science would bring man ever closer to the control of natural catastrophe. Art and culture could flourish. A temporal heaven would have been brought to earth.

To this vision of an earthly paradise, countless men have dedicated their lives. The dictatorship of the proletariat has lasted far longer in Russia than Marx probably envisioned, and longer than Lenin thought would be necessary. It has become a police state, resting on controls no longer related to the proletariat and often employed against them. These things have disillusioned many, and attracted others who see in Communism a way of personal aggrandizement, freed of moral restraint. The buccaneers driven long since from the waters of the world now sail the seas of politics, and fly the red flag as defiantly as their forebears raised the Jolly Roger.

But the basic hope, in which Marx sincerely died, is the hope which even now animates the most sincere of his followers, that mankind can create, indeed will be forced to create, a society freed of social evil, in which humanity may bring to fruition its age-old dreams and aspirations. It is this religious dimension of Communism which inspires its devotees with fanatical fervor and sacrificial dedication, and blinds them to the harsh realities of life in those nations where Communism is being tested and found grievously wanting.

The sun of Marxist hope gleams brilliantly on the horizon, and attracts the devotion of many who long for light; it is not until that sun has arisen that the worshippers find that Communist reality is, in the profound phrase of Arthur Koestler, "darkness at noon."

SUMMARY

In a letter written in 1852, Marx summed up what he believed was original in the *Manifesto,* and therefore in "Marxism": "What I did that was new was to prove (1) that the *existence of classes* is only bound up with particular, historic phases in the development of production; (2) that the class struggle necessarily leads to the *dictatorship of the proletariat;* (3) that this dictatorship itself only constitutes the transition to the *abolition of all classes* and to a classless society." (Quoted in Berlin, *Karl Marx,* p. 193.)

In the years that followed, and particularly after his death, the thought of Marx — like that of Hegel before him — gave rise to divergent streams, one moving toward moderate social criticism, and the other to violent revolution. The first stream is associated with the name of Edward Bernstein (1850-1932), who led the movement in Germany which sought by constitutional methods to achieve Marxist goals; the movement was named "Revisionism" by its critics, and Lenin bitterly attacked it in his *What is to be Done?* published in 1902. The other, radical stream was led by another German, Karl Kautsky (1854-1938) until he was eclipsed by Lenin (1870-1923), who not only discussed violent revolution but directed one.

The actual differences between these disciples, and among the many others who diverged more or less from the two major tributaries — the history of Marxism from its origins on into and after the Russian Revolution is a story of stormy and violent differences of opinion — were largely differences on how and when to bring a Communist society into being. Therefore no effort has been made in the preceding pages to discriminate shades and emphases in "Marxism," though these of course did, and do, exist. The enormous literature which has grown up to "explain" Marx shares enough common ground to permit the exposition and criticism of his leading themes as if they were universally asknowledged by his followers. A brief and illuminating discussion of the major divergencies may be found in Professor Hook's *Marx and the Marxists.*

CHAPTER 2

CAPITALISM, THE CLASSLESS SOCIETY, AND MAN

THERE IS NO POINT in pursuing a discussion unless you know what you want to defend and what ground you stand on. If we want to argue with a Marxist, we must know what capitalism is, and we must not try to beat the Marxist by standing on his ground.

BASIC PREMISES OF CAPITALISM

Capitalism is defined in as many ways, by as many writers, as is Socialism. No one's definition quite suits anyone else. Now, it is possible to wrangle, as do the semanticists, so long about definitions as to lose sight of the objects being defined. We will at least free ourselves to move on by defining capitalism as *a way of organizing society for the production of goods*. The organization arises from within, in relative freedom, upon individual initiative, and in considerable variety. These are the basic premises, or ideals, of capitalist society.

The first premise is that economic organization arises from within society. It is not imposed from without, or by an elite within. This involves the risk of haphazard organization, and overproduction of some commodities and no production of others.

The second premise is that human freedom is respected in the organization for production. Now, freedom involves the "right" to be (but not to stay) wrong. The abuse of freedom by those who acquire vast economic power creates hardship for others, and evokes intervention in some cases by the power of the state as representative of the whole people. But abuse of freedom emphasizes the reality of freedom. It is the risk freedom involves.

The third premise of capitalist society is that individual human ingenuity is the best way to solve economic problems.

The risk involved in this premise is that ingenuity may go to work against, as well as for, the common good. It is one of the wagers a society makes in letting ingenuity loose.

The fourth premise of capitalist society is that variety and flexibility best meet economic needs. Capitalized enterprise ranges from the rolling popcorn wagon to the rolling acres of industrial plant, and from tiny personal business to vast corporative enterprise. There is constant shift to meet changing environment. The risk involved in this premise is the tendency of mammoth corporations to grow still larger, threatening the very premise itself. Against this tendency the state must keep alert watch.

Capitalism is a way of organizing society for productive enterprise which takes risks in order to preserve ideals. The fact that the Marxist can point to grave failures is sad but instructive commentary upon the price freedom, initiative, flexibility and self-direction exact. It is on precisely these premises that hope for improvement rests. And it is because he denies these premises that the Marxist sees no hope for capitalism. But to do so, he has to blind himself to the massive strides capitalism has taken in correcting its own abuses since the days of Marx.

This, then, is what we defend. On this ground we stand. If we grasp the vital relation between freedom and failure, we will not be *dismayed* but *challenged* by every finger pointed at every shortcoming. We must take care, however, that we are not shifted to Marxist ground, where every shortcoming found in capitalism is cause for hatred and revolt.

What is the Marxist's ground? He accepts none of the capitalist premises. He doesn't believe that economic organization should arise from within a society, except in so far as the elite to whom he gives that power are also involved in the society they direct.

He doesn't really believe in human freedom. Man is the victim of material forces coming to expression in economics. Freedom is illusion. Man cannot dominate the laws of economics. The Marxist has no use for the "right" to be (even for a moment) wrong. To be wrong for a moment in Communist lands is frequently fatal.

Nor has he any faith in human initiative. He believes in control from the top, in patterns and plans. Marx insisted on "socially necessary" as a qualification of "labor" because he wanted the expenditure of labor power controlled and directed on a national level.

—— Nor does the Marxist care for flexibility. The massive organization reaching from top to bottom is his economic ideal, the whole made up of many cogs, each quite expendable.

What all this means is that the Marxist wants to take no risks. He believes that they will not be necessary in the classless society *because he believes there will be no evil in that society*. In a perfect society there need be no risks. There are no freedoms which need protection. Any organization for meeting economic needs will do.

The great difference, then, between capitalist society and Communist society is that the former recognizes social evil, and not that only, but human evil as well. It takes risks in order to allow the greatest possible freedom while reckoning with the inevitable influence of greed, selfishness, and, in short, sin.

And so, if we argue with the Communist on his ground, which is the unspoken assumption that a perfect society can be evolved on earth, he can always point to grave flaws in capitalism which we cannot often deny. They are the price we pay for our premises. But he denies the premises, and assumes that he will have no price to pay in consequence. In his anticipated classless society, he runs none of the risks which an imperfect society *must run* in order to secure limited realization of its ideals. And, therefore, on his ground he has the game all his own way: he finds capitalism full of faults, he admits to none of his own.

Be clear about it, before we begin our commentary on Marxism. If we insist that capitalism is perfect, we are lost. If we insist that it is, however wayward the results, *premised* on internal choices in meeting economic needs; that it is, however imperfectly, *premised* on human freedom; that it is, however underprivileged some of its children may be, *premised* on personal initiative; that it is, however powerful the trend toward monopoly in some industries may be, *premised* on flexibility and variety in enterprise — if, I say, we insist on these as indispensable in a world where human evil is real and operative, we stand on ground the Communist cannot effectively destroy.

And, finally, if we remember that capitalism is strong enough to permit criticism, encourage political democracy, and allow religious freedom, we know that it offers sound hope for vigorous struggle against social and personal evil as they come to manifestation. Denying all this, Communism must turn to its classless utopia in the hope that there man can slough off the evil which now entangles him.

CAPITALISM AND CRITICISM

These remarks about American capitalism have been construed by some as a eulogy of the system, and the author has been chided for reverencing it as a thing descended unblemished from heaven.

If, it may be said in reply, an attempt at the frank appraisal of those factors in the American political economy which have in fact permitted and provided an ever broader participation by the whole American people in the fruits of their industry is a eulogy, then a eulogy this will be. Moreover, if the paths by which this *broader* distribution of economic goods and services remain open — as they do — this fact cannot be emphasized and lauded enough.

An economic system exists for the purpose of organizing a nation's production and distribution of goods and services. There is no *a priori* reason why, and no state or economic law to mandate that, there should not be, in real fact, what once came to be symbolized by a slogan: a car in every garage (a garage for every family) and two chickens in every pot — all this provided by the American economy for every American family and many other families besides, by and under American capitalism. Whether this can come to pass on its own, so to speak, or will require ever more persistent nudges and assists from the state is largely up to Americans themselves.

Capitalism under a democracy is, I have tried to show, an open system, amenable to self-correction and state "partnership." In this *openness* resides its hope as well as its liability to abuse. If one wants the *hope* — my argument is — he has to risk (and reluctantly face in protean forms) the *abuse!* But the abuse then becomes his challenge, and the risk his opportunity! Men are not perfect, and their political economy will under any system but mirror them. The Christian concern is that it mirror less and less the worst and more and more the best — splitting the difference is not good enough — and that the system itself be open to continuous correction. Democratic capitalism is, I think, open to this kind of Christian criticism and amendment.

If, on the other hand, my eulogy suggests that in fact there *now* are — to keep the same symbols — cars in all American garages and in those of our sphere of international influence, and two chickens stewing daily and universally in savory pots; and that Christians have, therefore, nothing left to do but to contemplate the excellences of their capitalistic navels, then the thrust of at least a part of this book has been seriously misapprehended. A Christian economic program is not to be drawn from a hat, and is more spoken of than either drafted or acted upon, but it will find goals enough to strive to accomplish as long as it can get them concretely defined and generally supported. This task, by the way, I take to be a function of the study of economics in a Christian educational system. But this in passing.

There is little doubt that American capitalism has shown itself more amenable to self-correction, more sensitive to moral demands, and that it is more liable to the impression upon its ways of Christian patterns than is state socialism in any of its various forms. This does not mean that the American economy does not exhibit serious problems: its idle productive capacity, its seeming frustration with "plenty," its perplexities with automation, its threat of recession, its apparent dependence upon huge governmental military expenditures, its range of luxury-to-poverty, and other defects that as readily come to mind. But the attack upon these problems is not frustrated by fixed and rigid structural patterns sustained by the power of the state, as is more likely the case under state socialism and is indubitably the case under Communism.

Moreover, it is not to be denied, nor excused, that the relative openness of the American economic system has afforded the "robber barons" and their like the opportunity of foisting grotesque abuses upon American economic and political life. Nor is one to forget that the social legislation largely responsible for the melioration of abuses and the extension of general participation in the national wealth was enacted, and still is, in the face of bitter and relentless opposition waged in the name of capitalism itself.

Marx was wrong in supposing that none of the rich and powerful would voluntarily relinquish a part of his wealth and power — the latter is, on all levels of life, less easily given than the former — to the common good; but he was right in supposing that such voluntary contribution would not solve the major social problems of an industrial society. Where he erred the more seriously was in supposing that the power of the community exercised through its government would always devolve upon the side of the "haves" against the "have-nots," a mistake quite natural so long as he did not contemplate universal suffrage. The American "proletariat" got the ballot; the Russian "proletariat" got its dictatorship. The contrast between the liberties and influence enjoyed by the Americans and the restrictions and insignificance imposed upon the Russians is some measure of the aberration of Marxism in going for tyranny instead of for suffrage.

This contrast is ground for giving thanks to the Author of liberty. It is not meat for complacency. Malnutrition, insecurity, slums, disease, fear, still cry to heaven from dark corners of American urban wastelands. But the point here is: if we accept as a *challenge* the imperfections of American democratic capitalism, recognizing these imperfections as evidence of an openness in the system through which reforms as well as abuses can enter it, we may live and die in the free pursuit of the ideal; if, on the other hand, we dream of perfection and reject the realities under which we live in the name of such a dream, the price we pay for dreaming will be tyranny.

MARXIST "THEOLOGY"

It is no longer necessary to stress the many parallels which hold between Christianity and Marxism. This has become a common notion. Marx, in many ways, seems to have played the "sedulous ape" to Christian doctrine, in each instance substituting the natural for the supernatural, the material for the spiritual, and the human for the Divine.

Marxism rests, for example, upon the profound apprehension that the misery of man and the sickness of society are caused by the radical separation of man from ultimate reality. In form this understanding of the human situation parallels with amazing exactness the Christian doctrine that man's misery consists in his radical separation from God, the ultimate reality. Salvation consists, Christianity teaches, only in man's reunion with God, made possible in Jesus Christ. Having defined ultimate reality as material rather than Divine, Marx diagnoses man's misery as consisting in his separation from matter, in the form of the means of production. Salvation comes, Marx, teaches, when all men are reunited with material possessions in the common ownership of the means of production.

While parallel in form, Christianity and Marxism stand thus

in substantial opposition in their analysis of the root of evil and the way of salvation.

A brief sketch of the "theology" of Marxism would run as follows: the original sin occurred when man fell from the communal life of the nomadic tribe by acknowledging the right to private property in the means of production. From this sin followed all the evils of exploitation and struggle. Redemption from social evil can occur only when the original sin is undone, the private ownership of productive means is destroyed, and man is thus reunited with reality in the common possession of these means. Then only will exploitation cease, the dialectic come to an end, and man be enabled to enjoy the fruits of his own labor.

The redeemer is the proletariat. In its long suffering, the proletariat has earned the right to rebellion. (It might be stressed, in passing, that Marx uses "rebellion" where Christian doctrine would use "repentance." This is because Marx does not hold the proletariat responsible for its sins, a position fraught with significant consequences to be noted below.)

The day of judgment, in Marxist "theology," is that day of the revolution. And this, then, is heaven: the classless society in which man is freed from evil and able to emerge at last in the full flower of his potentialities.

What does this "theology" imply? It implies, first of all, that Marx recognized that unless some cure were found for human evil, mankind had no real hope of realizing its highest aspirations. Unless a social philosophy rested upon some kind of theology, and unless it were, in fact if not in theory, some kind of religion, it was finally doomed to disillusionment and disintegration. Without the classless society as its goal, Marxism is but another vigorous human attack upon a hopeless problem, the fact of evil in society. Like the formula for atomic fission, Marxism releases vast quantities of energy; but unless guided by the vision of a paradise, that energy is harmful, destructive and vain. Because the Marxist paradise is illusory, much of the energy it has released in history has been destructive. Its achievements in Russian technocracy, arts and letters have been made at the expense of the values of personality, freedom and spirit.

The second implication of Marxist "theology" is its abstraction. Evil arises out of the *form* of economic relations under which a society is organized. Evil can be eliminated, then, by changing the *form* of economic relations. Man is not involved in responsibility for the evil which he now does. It is, in effect, society which sins by countenancing the economic forms which drive men to evil. It is, in effect, society which will be saved when by revolution it destroys the economic forms. This is abstract evil and abstract salvation. Or, in other words, it is *formal* evil and *formal* salvation. Because this is so, Marxism tends to bring out that evil in man which roots, not in society, but in man himself.

If all this sounds far away from the concrete Marxism we discussed in the last chapter, be patient a while longer and continue reading.

EVIL AND SALVATION IN MARXISM

The ten of you who worked in the tea table factory are, before being employees, *men.* As men you crave freedom, purpose in life, some recognition, enough material possessions to live and raise your families in comfort, and, even though you might deny it, the unifying force of religion and the peace of resting in God.

Between you and these ends come many frustrations. Whether you analyze them as Marx did, or whether you analyze them in another way, they all embody one dark power: the power of evil in society, and in you and me. You are driven back, step by step, to the same ancient question *why?* For until we learn "why," our "how" will always be inadequate. And if our answer to the "why" is false, the false consequences in our everyday lives will be very real. For a slightly facetious example: the man who thinks that the solution to his life's problems is a wild spree, wakes up next morning with a big head and very bad taste. The "why" of his problems did not lie in his empty stomach, lack of liquor and starved passions. Because it did not, his "how" for overcoming his problems only resulted in more of them.

It is quite true that many ardent disciples of Marx may never think in terms of evil and salvation at all. But the awesome power of Marxism in the modern world is, at bottom, directly dependent upon the fact that it is, in reality, precisely directed upon the religious issues of life. The leadership knows that this is true, even if they, too, phrase it differently; the followers act upon it, even if they do not know its formulation. It is, as I have suggested, by the *translation* of a theory of evil and a proposal of its cure into the terms of everyday life that Marxism makes its appeal. It is our concern in this chapter to examine that theory, and attempt the translation of that examination, too, into the terms of everyday life.

The grave weakness in Marx's analysis of evil and its cure lies in the fact that he does not hold man responsible for his sin. In consequence, he can assure no man of his *personal* salvation, and from this follows the bitter struggle for survival which goes on in Communist nations. Marxism saves "man" but not "men." It saves society in general but no member of society in particular. This may be illustrated in several ways.

The concept of the classless society rests upon the change which the revolution will effect in the *form* of economic relations. From the form of private ownership of productive means, mankind must move to the form of common ownership of those means. That transition is, in Marxism, salvation.

This transition confers no promise as to who, in particular, will survive into the new classless society. It might be A, or B, or C; it could as well be X, or Y, or Z. Heaven comes into being when the economic *form* is changed. The question remains: who will be the saints? In Christian theology, the saints will be, paradoxically, precisely those who have sinned and recognized themselves as sinners. But in Marxist "theology" no person need recognize himself as a sinner. In consequence, no person is assured of his own salvation. This is the price he pays for having no personal sins to confess.

There might be, for all the Marxist can tell, but a fraction of the world's population left to enter the new order when at last it is assured. Marxism would, in fact, come to theoretical fruition if but *one* human being survived to become both owner and worker under the *form* of the classless society. If, perhaps, he could be kept from talking to himself, the class struggle would truly cease. Marxist salvation is abstract salvation, promised to all and guaranteed to none.

It is instructive to observe the practical consequences which follow upon this abstract doctrine of salvation. It accounts, first of all, for the singular indifference the Marxist exhibits for individual human lives, even, though it appears contradictory, his own. When society at large is the object of salvation, the concrete member of society may well (and often does) perish by the way. When the goal of the revolution is a change in the *form* of social life, the path which the revolution travels may well be over countless bodies of members of society. The final change in economic relations might as well be effected by one hand as by another.

In the second place, the abstract character of Marxist salvation accounts for the ruthless struggle for power which goes on within Communist nations and within the Communist Party everywhere. If society, in the abstract, is to be saved, the individual must make his part in that salvation sure by himself. If, say, one knows that an airplane is going to New York, this knowledge does him no personal good unless — if he wants to get to New York with the plane — he makes certain, by any means, that he is on board. In the same way, each Marxist believes in his heart, if he is sincere, that the classless society is written in the stars, and certain to arrive; but such knowledge does him personally no good unless he makes certain, by any means, that he survives into the new era. He might, of course (and this explains the seeming contradiction noted a moment ago), sacrifice his own life so that others he loves may enter the new world alive. But this simply illustrates the more vividly the extremes to which a man is driven who must make his own salvation, or that of others, secure. "What will a man give in exchange for his life?" He will exert every effort to keep it secure. The passionate struggle for power and position in Communism reflects the falsity of Marx's analysis of evil and its cure.

The grim brutality by which Stalin sought to assure his own survival was not, therefore, a deviation from Marxism. It was its moral consequence. Nor will his successors act otherwise. The man who has no personal sins to confess exacts from others the penalties for his own unforgiven crimes. He will have to make his own salvation sure by every means he can command, for he will find the source of evil outside himself and ever threatening his very life. And all the while the root of evil within him drives him to greater sins against his fellow men.

In the third place, the abstract character of Marxist salvation inspires the "new morality" which endorses every act which furthers the revolution, whatever that act may be. Whatever befalls the individual who seems to get into the way of the new order does not really matter, for that individual was never assured of salvation in the first place. The concepts of kindness, justice, honor, love and decency are meaningless in Communist morality because they concern the individual. In Communism the individual does not matter; all that matters is the *form* of the new society.

All told, the Marxist heaven is to the swift, the ruthless, and the cunning, who climb to it over the backs of their fellow Marxists and all others. Thus a defect in theory becomes a sinister threat in grim reality. Ideas *do* have consequences!

STALINISM

After all allowances have been made for the chaos which the Russian Communist Party inherited, and for the police brutalities which had long been a part of Russian life, it is still a question of crucial importance for the Marxist to inquire if exile, murder, and terror are or are not the logical and inevitable climax to the dictatorship of the proletariat. That is, if Stalinism, revealed in much, though not all, of its gruesomeness by Khrushchev's "secret speech" to the Twentieth Congress of the Communist Party of the Soviet Union, in spring 1956, is or is not inevitable before the classless society can be achieved. The exodus of Communist Party members around the world after the Khrushchev revelations suggests their grave misgivings on this score. It is a simple question to ask, and a decisive one: Is or is not Stalinism inevitable?

If not, then the next proletarian revolution, wherever it is brought about (China went to Stalinism at once), might be presumed to take a more humane road to its "paradise"; if so, and if Stalinism is a natural offspring of seeds sown in 1917, then the dream of a withering away of the state becomes tenuous indeed. For Stalinism was not directed at the bourgeoisie — they are, after all, in Marxist "demonology," legitimate prey — but it was directed at Party members once as active, or more so, than Stalin himself. Their "deviation" was defined by Stalin, and consisted largely in simple opposition to Stalin himself. This "Bonapartism," as the willful exercise of power was called, was courageously attacked by Trotsky; but the question is whether or not he was fighting, and finally became the murdered victim of, forces of history Lenin and he had themselves set in motion. This, of course, Trotsky denied. But supposing he had been victorious in his internal struggle with Stalin: might not the latter have forced him, by the nature of the context they had both helped to establish after October 1917, to employ equally "Bonapartist" methods to hold his position? Tyranny begets tyranny. If one should not, as Lenin advised, "dabble" at revolution, should he wanton with dictatorship and expect to cleanse his soul again?

At least Stalinism obliges the Marxist to face such questions. Having faced them, Howard Fast and other "comrades" could be Marxist no longer. There is, indeed, a certain blindness in us all, and the springs of our devotions are deep and hidden; but how blind, one wonders, must Communism really be if it can take the hideous travesty of Stalinism as on the road to Eden?

THE CLASSLESS SOCIETY

Let us suppose, however, that this analysis of Marxism is wrong. Let us imagine, then, that at least all Marxists do achieve membership in the classless society. Are they in a temporal heaven, freed of their sins?

What did Marx hold to be the cause of man's misery and evil? His alienation from reality, in the form of the means of production. What does the classless society promise him, then? His reunion with reality in the possession of the means of production. The promise of the Marxist heaven is that *society* will become the *owners* and the *workers* of productive enterprise.

The individual, however, is not society. In the classless society, it is not the individual but the community which will be reunited with productive property. This property becomes the possession of *all* . . . and *therefore,* ironically, the possession of *none*. What belongs to society as a whole, *for that very reason* belongs to no one in particular. The divorce between the individual and productive property is not healed by the classless society; it is rendered final and absolute! Man's misery is complete, if Marx is correct in analyzing the root of his misery as separation from productive reality.

If this seems a paradox (and perhaps it is) reflect on it for a moment. It is the Achilles' heel of Marxism.

Who *owns* a *public* building? Why, *everyone* does. Indeed, and precisely for that reason *no one* does! No Russian laborer can claim possession of the Russian industrial plant. Neither, by the same "dialectic," can he call even one bench, or one machine his "share." There are no shares in public property. He has no "shares" because, in theory, he owns it all. His ownership of *all* deprives him of ownership of *any*. What happens in Russia is, therefore, though the Marxists deny it, a logical consequence of Marxism. No one, in theory, owns any part of the productive enterprise, because, in theory, everyone owns it all. The misery of the proletariat in Russia illustrates the consequences of bad theory in practice.

The capitalism which the Marxist denounces, on the other hand, offers the individual an opportunity to own productive enterprise precisely because it denies that ownership to all. The price it pays is that some get far more than they need, and others suffer want. But, unlike the Marxist state, capitalism offers in its flexibility the opportunity for constant adjustment of evils. In the Marxist state the theoretical owners of all are frozen into their real positions of owning nothing.

The dictatorship of the proletariat is not only a euphemism for the real dictatorship of the ruthless few, but it is the final rather than the transition stage in Marxism. This position, for other reasons, was that taken by Stalin in the late years of his reign.

Obviously, in the classless society, the actual management of productive apparatus must be entrusted to those who "act" for the proletariat. The ownership of the many becomes embodied in the persons of a few. The prize tempts them to vicious struggle. The mystical notion that the many can actually "own" in an equal way finite objects, a notion as vague as Rousseau's "general will" of the people, can finally be defined only in what results from it. The result is that there is constant struggle for the position to act in the name of the many, a struggle made all the more ruthless by the extent of the power to be achieved.

The profound alienation of man from reality, which, properly defined, is indeed his misery, is neither healed in the revolution nor bridged in the classless society. Marxism is a false religion. Like all falsehoods it brings suffering in its train.

Let us suppose, however, that all which has been argued so far is denied, and imagine that the classless society does come into being as Marx envisioned it. What then?

We must remember that the Communist is chary in his discussion of the exact nature of the classless society — he has his reasons, which will be discussed in the next chapter — but Marx gave the classic theoretical formulation of its economic intention in his "to everyone according to his need. . . ."

Let us suppose that some reasonable and acceptably fair arrangement were devised to operate the commonly owned means of production. It would have to be at a national level in order to obtain the "socially necessary" employment of labor power. It could not be democratically conducted, as Marx seemed to wish, and Lenin maintained was true, because the allocation of "socially necessary" labor power cannot be decided by a show of

hands. Further, if each industry sought to control itself democratically, there would arise that competition between units
which would threaten to start the dialectic spiral on its way
once more. That the employees can earn ownership in an industrial enterprise and share in its dividends and in its policies is
possible under the flexibility of capitalism. Under the classless
society, it would be a threat to stability.

For this reason, Russia offers the only analogy in the modern
world to what the classless society might be like. No comparison
with the public ownership of selected instruments in economic
life as occurs in democratic capitalism could be precise, for these
by no means have the hold on the national economy which the
"ruling committee" would exercise, and does exercise, in Communist society. For this reason, also, the entrance of the state
into economic ownership is not Communism. So long as it is
limited strictly to those tasks for which the state is best fitted, it
serves rather to strengthen the national economy, promote private enterprise, and serve the general welfare.

The assumption that "labor value" would measure the true
reward which each workman received for his work in the classless society was surrendered by Marx even as he advocated it.
"To each according to his need" is the confession that no accurate measure can be constructed which would convert into actual
practice the abstract theory that all kinds of labor can be reduced
to a common unit. Marx does not deny that the real value which
labor confers upon raw materials cannot really be measured,
and that therefore the *real value* of a tea table cannot be compared *scientifically* with the *real value* of a refrigerator, to say
nothing of the *real value* of medical therapy or fine art. The
labor theory of value, therefore, becomes a revolutionary slogan
rather than an economic reality. To avoid, therefore, the inevitable disputes which would arise concerning the worth of one
man's labor as compared to that of another, Marx cuts the knot
by recommending distribution of goods according to need.

But human need is infinite, and man is infinitely capable
of *demonstrating* (to his own satisfaction) that each need must
be met, and at once! Marx's program presupposes, therefore, an
unlimited supply of goods of all kinds, an extraordinary self-
discipline among those who have to wait their turn, and a
super-human wisdom among the unhappy few who have to
superintend the division of goods "according to need." The

classless society would not make men saints; it would presuppose sainthood.

Let us go one further step, and suppose that these economic difficulties were also overcome, and that the mythology of Marxism was realized on earth. There would be, first of all, a plenitude of goods.

So widespread is wealth of possessions, especially in the Western world, that mankind has already, in many places, this plenitude of goods. Yet instead of reaping joy and peace from having "according to his need," the owner of these possessions as often as not harvests astounding boredom, against which he contrives endlessly unsatisfying pleasures. If all that the classless society can promise its members is endlessly increased and varied production and distribution of things, all it finally guarantees is satiety and boredom. Yet what can materialism offer which is *real*, other than things, for by definition matter is, for materialism, the only reality?

Perhaps it is recalled that the classless society offers mankind the first opportunity really to enjoy his possessions in freedom from struggle and freedom from evil. He then has *real* freedom. Apart from the difficulty of defining what *real* freedom could be in a materialist's world, it may be noted that man long ago declared his "real freedom" from governing forces, and what he has freely obtained in exchange is anxiety, misery, and fear. From the Garden of Eden to the German *Uebermensch*, men have asserted their independence, and found anxiety. Never does a man feel so alone as when he whistles most bravely against the universal dark which surrounds him when he is "free." The courageous figure holding aloft the candle of comradeship and learning in an otherwise empty world — according to Bertrand Russell's conception of it — is not so much heroic as histrionic. He plays not so much the king of the court as the jester. For his candle illuminates nothing, his learning lays hold of nothing, because his destiny is nothing. Freedom for its own sake is indeed "dreadful freedom," but it is more: it is *slavery*.

There is, finally, the possibility that the classless society might rise above its assumptions and embrace spiritual goods like art, learning and what is called culture. But the idea of culture, in all its highest reaches, rests not only on spiritual foundations but also suggests the transcendent and timeless in a way which would mock the temporality of the classless order. Only on the assumption that with other evil would go also old age and death, so that classless man lived in time forever, would the idea of culture cease to hold terrors for him. Otherwise, the fact that culture embodies the idea of the infinite would mean that *his own culture* would *mock classless man's finiteness*. Fine art, for example, is suffused with the timeless. The perfection of a sonnet, or of a painting or piece of sculpture, quite defies the time and space of its setting. The "return" from the enraptured experience of losing oneself in music is a "coming-back" into time and space out of neither. Art is disciplinary by subjecting man to the significance of the eternal, or it is simply evocative of man's own reaction and confronts him with only himself. If it does this, as much of modern art seems to attempt to do, it becomes erratic, propagandistic, and meaningless. Either, then, fine art would mock the classless man, or it would cease to be art.

The whole concept of culture, in its spiritual sense, is incompatible with the idea of a finite man, in any society. The classless society could endure it only if somehow that society achieved eternity in time. The more sensitive men became, the more they would, otherwise, ask questions like these: if I am doomed to die tomorrow, even though that tomorrow be deferred a thousand years, *why survive today?* Shall I enjoy art? *Art mocks me!* Shall I be free? *Freedom terrifies me!* Shall I accumulate goods? *Accumulation bores me!* Shall I exalt myself, then, in one final act of self-assertion against it all? Ah, yes, in one act of exaltation against the universal nothingness: *suicide!* (as Dostoevsky works out in his novel *The Possessed*).

In Christian terms, heaven without God is . . . hell!

EVIL AND SALVATION IN CHRISTIANITY

In contrast with the Marxist view of sin and salvation, Christian doctrine is that it is the *individual* who sins, and *therefore* it is the *individual* who, upon confession, repentance, and Divine forgiveness, is saved.

Marx would have dismissed this statement, of course, as merely "the translation of an ordinary question into less intelligible language." Without asking if there are any "ordinary" questions which can be answered without implicating spiritual values which Marx would have ruled out as unintelligible, we may pay him tribute for a certain neatness of method. An easier way of avoiding an objection might be hard to find.

Marx, and the whole evolutionary tradition to which he belonged, thought of this Christian conception of man as blackest pessimism. What Marx and those of his tradition did not recognize is that without individual acceptance of responsibility for sin there can be no assurance of individual salvation. Man does not personally escape the consequences of evil until he recognizes that he is personally responsible for the evil which he does, and is by this recognition induced to turn within for its cause, and to God for its cure. When he finds the root of all evil within his own soul, he is ready to turn for its eradication to that Spiritual Power which alone can reach into the soul itself.

Jesus dealt rarely with man in general, and frequently with man in particular. How often His parables begin with, "And a certain man. . . ." Christianity is pre-eminently the religion of the "certain man." It has been called the most individualistic of religions, because it teaches that a general salvation for all turns out to be particular salvation for none. Christ is the Hope of the *world* only and precisely because He is the Savior of *each sinner who in his personal particularity turns to Him.* Each person who accepts Christ's divine (for if not divine, then absurd) invitation, "Come unto Me . . . ," finds rest unto *his* soul in so far as he personally meets the Person of the Savior.

When the individual, in all his particularity, recognizes himself as sinner and finds in Christ *his* Savior, then to that individual the Spirit speaks the assurance of Saint Paul, "For I am persuaded, that neither death, nor life, nor angels, nor principalities, nor powers, nor things present, nor things to come, nor height, nor depth, nor any other creature, shall be able to separate us from the love of God, which is in Christ Jesus, our Lord." This is the assurance the Christian obtains, not for having sins to confess, but for having confessed his sins.

God, as Francis Thompson so vividly depicts in his *Hound of Heaven,* strips the individual of all his associates, of each pretense, of each cloak, of each evasion until the one meets the One, alone. And having met him thus, God saves him forever. On this individualism rests real hope. Beside it the Marxist mystical vision of a general salvation for society is but a pale abstraction.

Far indeed from underestimating the nature and worth of a man, Christianity is the only secure validation of both. It is in Christian doctrine, and not in Marxism or evolutionary optimism, that every man (including you, reader, and me) is recognized as a living, everlasting creature, whose incalculable worth is the result of his creation and sustenance by, and destiny in

God. Man can be the source of evil in the world only and exactly because he was created the crown of God's works. Only as lord of creation could man by his personal sin rend that whole creation and subject it to "groaning and travail to this very hour." So deeply, so radically was the wound of sin inflicted by man's own act, and so significant was man to God, that only in God's becoming man could the thralldom be broken. Only thus could begin the restoration of man to his original status in a creation once again to be made whole by the Creator's redeeming love.

This is the misery, and the grandeur, of man. Only one who began so high could fall so low; and only one fallen (by his own confession) so low can aspire to his once regal eminence. This is the source of the visions of the paradise which the Marxist measures in material terms and destroys in seeking to realize by himself. Man has latent memories of having come from the hand of his Creator destined for lordship over that creation to which dialectical materialism seeks to subject him. As heir to living bread he is victimized by that false religion which awakens the hunger only to satisfy it with a stone. It is to those who belatedly learn that their souls cannot feed upon stone, however multiplied, that Christ extends His hand still, opening the door of hope, the way of beatitude, offering Himself, "the living bread come down from heaven." It is only in Him that the hopes stirred and enlivened by the false promise of earthly paradise may come at last to the fruition for which they are given.

It is from Christian roots, then, that mankind may expect the "fruits of the spirit." There need be no competition for heaven, or for place in heaven. All of the moral values which protect the worth of the individual receive religious sanction. There is blessing enough for all. There is, as the Reformers stressed, the calmness of assurance that none of God's own can drop out of His hand. Unlike the fruits of Marxism, the fruits of Christian faith unite, strengthen the weak, protect the frail, and draw men together.

Not only is Marx's conception of the true misery of man, as alienation from reality, a close parallel to that of Christianity, but the Marxist intuition that redemption must have social consequences is also a reflection of Christian doctrine. Wrong as Marx was in trying to assure individual men of salvation by the promised salvation of society, he only reversed a profound Christian truth, often neglected: the salvation of men has inescapable social implications in time, that is, here and now.

There have been those, and they are common still, who deny the social relevance of Christianity. Let the Church tend the saving of souls, they maintain, and meddle not with other affairs, particularly with the affairs of economics, where the cleric's views are likely to be visionary and unrealistic. While the precise relation of the Christian Church as institute to economics is complex and disputed, the relation of the Church member to social problems of all kinds is clear. He is under the mandate of his Lord, stimulated by the preaching of the Word of God, to bring all things, starting with his own life, and including the world of economics, into subjection unto Him.

Those who hold that Christianity is limited to the saving of *souls* ignore the fact that Christianity is the religion of body and soul in indissoluble unity. They ignore the relevance of redemption for history, a relevance derived not only from the doctrine of creation, but also from the Incarnation, the resurrection, and the bodily ascension of Christ. Redeemed man is freed from the toils of time when his Master calls him, and until then he must play his part in history as *redeemed man*. Salvation has personal consequences, and these become social consequences as the saved sinner moves in his environment. The scorn which the critics of Christianity heap upon professing Christians arises in part because the latter exert so little influence upon society in the name of their Lord.

The Christian, wrote Abraham Kuyper, should not rest until the social order offers all men an existence worthy of man. If the Christian's relationship with his risen Lord is *real*, it will have real consequences in history. Just as the measure of the unreality of the Marxist scheme of social salvation is revealed by the miseries which it introduces wherever it is tried, so the measure of the reality of the Christian's personal redemption is the extent to which faith becomes works. Those who seek to deny the relevance of Christianity to society are those who do not understand the power of the Spirit. "If these should be silent, the very stones would cry out!" If faith is real, life both personal and social is changed. We will return to this matter in a later chapter.

THE CHRISTIAN DOCTRINE OF PROPERTY

It is in Marxism, too, that there echoes sound Christian doctrine regarding the ownership of property. For it must be remembered that the Marxist attack upon private property *now* is to the end that *later* all men may share it. Marx's failure in this regard is in attempting to secure the ownership of property equally for all, and thus assuring it to none.

This appreciation of the worth of property to man, upon which so much of Marxism rests, is an ancient part of Christian doctrine. Except for the sects, which sought to communalize property, the Church has always defended the right of private ownership of property, both personal and in productive means. Christianity is, said Archbishop Temple, the most materialistic of religions.

Unlike Marxism, however, Christianity recognizes the value of private property not in its possession so much as in its use. Thus the main stream of Christian teaching has held that man has no *absolute* right in his possession of private property. This separates Christian doctrine from classical economics. God grants man the right to property, as He grants him talents and the freedom to use them, only that it may be employed for divine ends. "There cannot be imagined a more certain rule," writes Calvin, "or a more powerful exhortation to the observance of it, than when we are taught that all the blessings we enjoy are divine deposits, committed to our trust on this condition, that they should be dispensed for the benefit of our neighbors." And, further, ". . . whatever God has conferred on us, which enables us to assist our neighbor, we are stewards of it, and must one day render an account of our stewardship."

The Christian doctrine of property exhibits three aspects.

First, it is recognized that personal property is an important element in the self-development of a person, in the unfolding of individuality into personality. The self finds itself reflected in belongings, in the things which one has acquired by his effort. This, you will recall, was the basis of Marx's doctrine of alienation. Further, the self develops moral power in the use of goods. Freedom is exercised and disciplined in the acquisition and disposition of personal property. In recognition of this intimate relation of property to personality, Chritianity has long defended the right to its possession and use. Except for the extremes of asceticism, Christianity has allowed for the enjoyment of one's possessions, always coupled with the warning that the stewardship of goods will be judged by a righteous Judge.

Second, the Church has long recognized the value of personal property and productive property as a bulwark of individual freedom. Not only, as already suggested, that freedom is, so to speak, practiced in the use of things, but also that he who has the resource of property is so far forth independent of economic pressures which may be brought to bear against his liberty, his social life, and his religion. The form which security is beginning to take in modern life is that of economic guarantees in wages, in unemployment insurance, disability benefits and pensions. All of these are extending to those whom Marx called the proletariat a far higher degree of personal security than they have enjoyed before. Such guarantees effect in principle what the Church has long defended as a paramount blessing of private property, namely, the assurance of freedom, including also that freedom from fear which conduces to peace of mind and soul. The Church has always endorsed the right to private property as a resource against tyranny. The Church through its members should have something positive to say for the movement toward economic security in highly industrialized nations.

3   Finally, and most important, the Church has always recognized the right to private property, personal and productive, as indissolubly related to the life of personal charity. One man's gift to another brings into reality the love which the one bears toward the other. For where love is properly defined as a settled design for another's good, rather than as some stirring of the heartstrings, it is in giving that this love comes to overt and historical expression. Charity is not, of course, the only expression of love, but nonetheless it is in the actual gift, given in love, that one man's desire for another man's good is also brought out of the realm of the potential into the realm of the actual. By thus making the word of charity into the deed of charity, Saint James teaches, faith becomes realized. In the miracle of charity, both the giver and the receiver are, as Shakespeare has it, blessed. Private property becomes the means by which the giver has enlarged, and in a deep metaphysical sense, *realized* his soul while enriching the receiver in his need. History thus becomes, so to speak, the forecourt of eternity; the soul which is *realized* in *acts* of charity is the soul which enters eternity forever.

For this reason, the early Christian fathers taught that the poor were God's *gift* to the rich, God's opportunity for those who possessed goods to exercise due stewardship over them, and in so doing "possess their souls." The gift represents in concrete historical form man's love for his neighbor, just as the God-man

Christ represented in concrete historical form the love of God for men.

Nor is this opportunity limited to those of great wealth. The sublime truth taught by the gift of the two mites is that charity is realized as fully in the small as in the great gift. Indeed, Jesus measured the two mites as of more value than the bags of gold.

But, and this is the point here, both the two mites and the bag of gold must have been the property of the givers in the first place. No gift can realize one's love unless it is first *his*, under God, to keep or to give as he decides. He must be *free*. The goods must be *his*. For both rights the Church has always firmly stood. But it has also recognized in both these rights, property and freedom, gifts which God validates only as the possessor of them employs them for the welfare of the community. In a sense, the Church fathers taught, property is God's grant to man in exchange for services he renders through it to his neighbor. In this light they taught that alms are not so much charity as justice.

CHRISTIAN STEWARDSHIP

In the light of this view of property and personality, property and freedom, and property and charity we may understand the profundity of Marx's analysis of the misery of the proletariat. Those who have nothing to call their own beyond the means of bare subsistence are deprived of much that is instrumental to personal development and religious life. The man who has to sell his labor power, that is, himself, solely in order to survive, with no hope of acquiring property and security, does not enjoy the life which Christianity recognizes as distinctively human. He cannot live at its best the kind of life which Christianity recognizes as of eternal significance.

But this misery is not, as Marx supposed, to be healed by the abstract union of man with property in utopia. It is to be healed by the dominion of Christ over the realm of economics; by the practical recognition that "the laborer is worthy of his hire." It is to be healed by the recognition by employer and employee alike that each is steward of his talents and possessions, and that the one is entitled to a day's labor, and the other to a day's wages. It is to be healed by the practical application to daily life of Saint Paul's teaching that the distribution of gifts and the variety of personal talents which God has ordained among men is to the end that each might share with the others in forming one living *body* together.

To each individual has been left the awful responsibility of determining what his stewardship shall be, in the sure knowledge that one day he will render to a just Judge an account to the least item of what he has done with his talents. In this ineluctable fact lies one source (the other is the complementary aspect of God's love) of the power of Christian social criticism. Herein, and not in revolutionary plotting, resides the power to overcome evil. Only the *power* of God can overcome the *power* of evil.

The testing time is short. After that comes the Judgment. It is popular these days to lift the eyebrows a trifle at the "crudities" of a sermon like Jonathan Edwards's "Sinners in the Hands of an Angry God." Those who do not deny its implication altogether, prefer C. S. Lewis's more sophisticated (and perhaps in its modern context more persuasive) suggestion that the sinner unfits himself for heaven, and finds, symbolically, that the soft grasses there lacerate his feet. The terrible reality, however expressed, remains the same: time is the testing ground for the quality of man's stewardship of all the gifts, personal and material, with which God has endowed him. And *after* the testing, the *Judgment!* "God is not mocked. Whatsoever a man soweth, that shall he also reap." Then he that hath spiritually acquired ten pounds will be richly rewarded; and he that hath selfishly turned to no account the gift of his Lord will lose even that which he had.

Infected by a little popular Freudianism, perhaps, the modern Christian depreciates fear as a source of dynamic. He forgets Augustine's reminder that to flee God pleased, is to meet Him displeased. He forgets that the power of the threatened Marxist revolution, which has much of free mankind chattering in terror, resides in the fear it inspires. Yet compared with the Judgment of God its threat fades into inconsequence. Jesus, who cared less for Freudianism and more for realities, did not hesitate to touch upon fear as a well-spring of conduct. "But I forewarn you whom ye shall fear: Fear him, which after he hath killed hath power to cast into hell; yea, I say unto you, Fear him."

If the Church has lost much of its power to influence social and personal behavior, it is because the Church has lost touch with some Christian realities. The medieval woodcuts with the eye of God prominently etched at the top of the picture conveyed to their time a conception the modern world "wists naught of." God sees even the secret dealings and the inmost thoughts. The angel with pen in hand bending over a large volume to record each man's deeds went out of style with the kind of painting which featured him. But the truth remains.

The Church courts its own weakness if it does not declare from pulpit and from housetop that property which is not stewarded according to God's commands is property over which its owners, temporal and temporary, do well to "weep and howl." If the Church does not denounce with the voice of the Prophets the neglect of the poor, and if it obscures by subtle exegesis what the Bible says about possessions and their use in love, it loses in power in direct proportion as it dilutes its mandate.

The nineteenth-century Church lost the working class, as Pope Pius XI expressed it, because it lost touch with the revealed will of God. Power flows only through open lines. It is a serious and humbling question to inquire why in the councils of the nations the voice of the Church as it comes to overt expression in the teaching of the Church and the conduct of its membership is so feebly heard and so little acknowledged. And if, as occurred in the Middle Ages, the Church in an effort to bolster its spiritual inadequacy turns to secular power as a substitute for its own lack of spiritual force; if in deference to Mammon, it renders unto Caesar the things which are God's, its spiritual bankruptcy is reflected in its social insignificance.

The power of Christianity as a social force for righteousness — in the world of economics too — resides in the truth of Christianity as a doctrine. The Church mumbles in the councils of the nations today because it has lost touch with the sovereign power and truth of the *Scriptures,* and the living Christ revealed in them.

The Christian doctrine is, clearly, what Marx never quite understood, that property is never an end in itself. Just as Marx could not bring himself to believe that personal salvation can come only after confession and repentance by the same person, so also he could not conceive that self-realization through the possession of property comes only through disciplined enjoyment and charitable employment of it. Christian teaching is emphatic that the endless acquisition of things as ends in themselves does not enable the soul to find itself, but in fact disperses, divides, and well-nigh destroys it. To gain the whole world might well be, in very truth, to lose one's own soul in the process.

It is not in the gaining, but in the using of goods, both for his own development and that of others, that man realizes his soul through private property. Property as an end in itself is no more a liberating force than poverty; and in comparison of the two, the Church has always commended the latter. Property accumulated without the intention of its use to spiritual ends is, indeed, property in the Marxist sense; and because it is, it will assert its dominion over the soul precisely because it is valued more highly than the soul. For if a man will not see in his possessions the opportunity to serve his own spiritual development and the lives of others, his possessions will exact service from him. The evidence that such is the "dialectic" of property in its relation to man is all about us.

The same inexorable "dialectic" may be observed in the relation of thought to matter since the days of Descartes. In Descartes, man discovered himself, not in self-denial but in self-affirmation, and he guaranteed his own reality, not in self-sacrifice, but by his own act of thought. "I think, therefore I am." From his own affirmed existence, man derived the existence of God and things. Because, in a sense, man "made" things, he could call them his own, absolutely, and do with them as he pleased, as long as he injured no other creature who also carried the world about by his act of thought.

But man was unable to sustain the world and God by this selfish possession of them. And in philosophical materialism, things took their revenge and claimed possession of man, leaving him but another kind of matter in motion, from which even his act of thought was derived. Thus, while Decartes had derived the world from the existence of thinking man, Marx derived thinking man from the existence of the world. Man, who had chosen to make a world after his own image, found himself become the slave of the world he had made, a pawn in the grasp of forces he can at best, according to Marx, seek to foresee and understand. In the same manner, the person who treats his possessions as absolutely his own, denying that he has any responsibility to the God who made both him and them, ends by becoming the worried, tired slave of the things to which he has given, really, his own life.

Even if, therefore, Marxism could guarantee an endless supply of goods to the inhabitants of the classless society, these goods would dominate rather than liberate the energies of those who "possessed" them. If, as Christ taught, life is found only in losing it, then matter is likewise possessed only in giving it away, in committing it to God and neighbor in love.

The misery of the true proletariat, of whom there are increasingly few in the Western world, is that they have no property to possess; the misery of the citizen of the classless society is that he cannot take possession of the property he "has"; the misery of the owner of property is that he lives in constant danger that his property will take possession of him. True freedom comes when a man dedicates all that he has to the service of his Lord; only then does he come into real possession of all the things he has, "as having nothing, yet possessing all things." "For all things are yours; whether Paul, or Apollos, or Cephas, or the world, or life, or death, or things present, or things to come; all are yours; and ye are Christ's; and Christ is God's." In Christ the believer possesses all things, and yet nothing can separate him from the love of God. For possessions no longer threaten his relation to God, after he has surrendered them to His service, and thus taken a new possession of them not only, but of the very world itself. It is thus that Christianity fulfills the hope falsified by Marxism, and unites man with the world because he has first been united with God. This is the reality of the mystical possession of all by each, which Marxism fails to achieve because it translates it into the world of materialism, where spiritual possession is unreal.

"Seek ye first the kingdom of heaven, and then all these things shall be added unto you." This is the Christian defense of property, which is neither Marxist nor that of classical economics. This is the right the Church has to speak to the world of enterprise.

Life and men being what they are, however, it happens that some Communists (and it is idle to inquire how many) who expressly *deny* the existence and power of God, do in practice works of uncommon devotion, courage, and self-denial; while some Christians (and it is equally idle to inquire how many) who expressly *affirm* the existence and power of God, do in practice works of uncommon selfishness. This, I say, has to be acknowledged.

The distinguished French Catholic philosopher, Jacques Maritain, suggests in his *True Humanism* that God, who could so completely deny Himself on Golgotha, could clothe Himself also in the Communist's denial to empower secretly their deeds of charity. He believes that there will be on that "youngest day" of Final Judgment "surprised" Christians — both those who thought they never knew Jesus the Christ, and those who find that He has never really known them. But we do not need to accept or deny this kindly speculation of Professor Maritain's in order to be shamed into self-analysis both by Communist "charity" and Christian dereliction.

Life is not funded, finally, only upon precise intellectual distinctions; verbal victories over Communist ideology are worth while only when they contribute to Christian attempts to solve in practice the social problems which called Marxism into being. What we can learn from Communists who seem to act like Christians, and from Christians who seem to act like Communists, is that deeds count, and that words without deeds hardly matter at all. Faith without works is simply dead.

CHAPTER 3

HISTORY AND UTOPIA

THOUGHT IS BESET by paradox. Because the Marxist denies paradox, that is, humanly, the equal ultimacy of the logically contradictory, he is incapable of observing what it does to his own thinking. He does not grasp, therefore, the paradoxical relation which heaven has to history.

To put the problem in two sentences which it will be the purpose of this chapter to expound:

(1) The Marxist, whose eye is fixed on an earthly paradise, refuses, paradoxically, to be bound by the study of history at all.

(2) The Christian, whose eye is fixed on his Savior in heaven, reckons, paradoxically, in grave earnest with temporal history.

This is the way it is. In Marxist theory it is supposed to be precisely the opposite. The Marxist believes that he takes history in dead earnest, while his opponents in general, and Christians in particular, ignore it. This is because he denies paradox. He could not understand, for another instance, that Christians can sincerely hold that (1) man is free and morally responsible for what he does, and (2) God is sovereign and controls all things, including man, by His providence. Both, the Christian says, are true. We must live by both, until that day when we no longer see through a glass darkly.

To return to the problem of the chapter, it is important to have a "feel" for the term *history*. Much of modern thought, especially since Hegel and Darwin, involves the idea of history. It is best not to think of history as a miscellaneous collection of wars, kings and memorable dates, with a bit of adventure and romance tossed in to relieve the monotony. This is rather precisely what *history*, as used now, does not mean.

It is better to think of history as a flowing stream including simply everything. All events, all persons, war and peace, love and hate, customs and manners, work and play, men famous and men infamous all related together in a vast pattern ever changing in the past and ever growing forward out of today into tomorrow: that is history — the ideas of development and of unity working together to make one whole out of the living, moving, changing avalanche of life on this planet, in which all events are interrelated, man to man, man to nature, and man to God. History is, in another way still, that drama in which you and I and all persons and things play our parts each ticking moment of our lives.

It is this history which the Marxist assumes to take seriously, and really does not. It is this history which the Christian is presumed not to take seriously and really does. This is not just an interesting paradox. It is the reason why Christianity has been a powerful positive force toward social progress, while Marxism has been a powerful disruptive force toward social disintegration. Flaws in theory, as we have seen before, have consequences in practice.

THE CLASSLESS SOCIETY AND HISTORY

Now, Marx always insisted that he derived his system from a careful study of history. Marxists are fond of insisting that they think "concretely," which means they always stick to the facts. That this is not really the case may be shown by an illustration.

Let us suppose that a student of Marxism grasps the truth that the concept of the classless society, the earthly paradise, is not only the capstone of Marxist theory but is also the capstone of Marxist propaganda. It is this vision which distinguishes Marxism from other forms of violent social criticism, like, say, anarchism, which has never been a serious contender for men's allegiance. Sensing, then, that Marxism draws much of its propaganda appeal, both consciously and unconsciously, from the concept of a perfect society, the critic begins to examine that idea in some detail.

He finds, first of all, as we have noted, that the Marxist is very vague about the whole notion of the classless society. Marx hardly discussed it systematically. Lenin generalized about it, and Stalin was much too busy explaining its delayed arrival to wish to theorize concerning it. If the critic presses the matter, and asks for more detail, he learns that the Communist draws no blueprints of the classless society *now*. Why? Well, basically because he cannot. Why not? Because it is impossible to do so in current language and thought-forms. Once more, why not? Because the very concepts and language which men now employ are fashioned by the environment of class struggle out of which they, like all spiritual forms, arise. Our very habits of thought are conditioned by class struggle. This is true because, Marx taught, matter always controls the forms of logic, psychology, and language. This is simply materialism.

Therefore the language, logic, and thought-forms of history as we live it cannot apply to the new society, where there will be no struggle. Thought-forms on this side of the revolution do not apply to life on the other side. History has in this sense no claim on the classless society — the same history, of course, from which Marx claimed to draw his certainty that the classless society would be achieved.

Suppose, in the second place, that the critic insists that there must be something to be learned about the classless society on this side of the revolution, and points out that the Marxist himself does, after all, talk and think about it. And suppose that the critic proceeds to argue that communist experiments have been tried and found wanting, and communal enterprises have often failed; he then tries to apply the causes of these failures, as he understands them, to the idea of the classless society. What then?

He finds that the Marxist rejects abruptly all analogies drawn from history. Why? Because the classless society is, you will recall, strictly speaking beyond history. History as we know it, governed by the dialectic and conducive to struggle, will cease when the classless society comes into being. This being so, all argument drawn from present history cannot apply to post-history, to the classless society. The Marxist will not be bound by the lessons of history, the same history which is supposed to validate Marxism.

In the third place, the critic tries another tack. He turns to the Communist state of Russia, and seeks to interpret the classless society in terms of what Russia has done since 1917. He is met at once with the "irrelevance" of this criticism. Russia, he is told, is as yet but a semi-redeemed part of a predominantly bourgeois and therefore enemy world. The really Communist society will not — Trotsky said *could* not — begin until all nations accept Marxism, or have it forced upon them. Russia, Stalin often argued, is surrounded by foreign foes without and threatened by foreign agents within, and therefore the pattern of true Marxism is distorted and its development impeded. The Communist refuses to accept Russian Communist history as normative for the classless society. Lessons drawn from it are not binding for the new order.

Or, finally, the critic draws one last arrow from his quiver. He seeks to project conclusions drawn from the nature of man himself into the new society. If man is like *this,* then in the classless society he must react like *that,* and so on. Briskly the Communist reminds him that the only "man" history knows is the victim of class struggle, whether he be of the proletariat or of the bourgeoisie. This kind of man will not exist in the classless society. Therefore any inference drawn from the one kind of man will not necessarily, or even probably, apply to the other. In judging the classless society, the Marxist accepts no responsibility to what history or introspection teach concerning the nature of mankind.

In summary, the Marxist denies that any aspect of history as we now know it can be used as a standard of judgment in the discussion of the classless society. This places him in an enviable argumentative position, or, rather, this removes the concept of the classless society out of the realm of argument altogether. The idea of the classless society becomes amorphous enough to be all things to all Marxists, and nothing to all critics. Between it and history there is, in reality, no logical passage at all. On this subject the Communist and the anti-Communist volley their charges over a bottomless gulf — the chasm which divides history from post-history.

This *chasm* between the dispensations is important. It represents for Marxism (though no Marxist puts it so) that *hill* which in *Pilgrim's Progress* is where the great burden of historical evil drops away. This infinite gulf between history and the classless society is for Marxism the unintentional recognition that man must pass through the infinite, in some sense, before he can enter "heaven." The complete break which Marxist theory makes between history and the new society means, in fact, that man as he is will never get into the new world unaided.

It is quite inconceivable how a Marxist who lived before and through the revolution could enter the classless society. How could he, in reality, put on the "new man" in lieu of the man who had been formed by all the tensions of class struggle? And if he brought into the new society any of the vestiges of the old, they could become germs from which evil might once more develop.

It is provocative how closely the Marxist position parallels Christian doctrine. It is Christian teaching that nothing of history shall enter *unchanged* into heaven. It is Marxist doctrine that nothing of history pertains to the classless society. But in Christianity the "new man" of heaven will be the "old man" reborn. The continuity is not broken. This rebirth, however, is not the work of the man, but the work of God.

Marxism, based as it is on philosophical materialism, has no concept of rebirth. At some point in history, the same persons who make the revolution, who staff and support the dictatorship of the proletariat, are supposed to enter the classless society. The fact that that process is presumed to be gradual obscures but does not lessen the tension which holds between things of "this" history and things of "that" post-history. The Marxist who makes that fateful crossing from history into post-history would leave his very self behind, for that self has been nurtured on the thought, the logic, the passions, the struggles, and the material realities of history. Without these, what *kind* of self, on Marxist grounds, remains? What happens to these selves which are but the reflections of matter in configuration, when that configuration is radically altered? In each of the previous periods of history, as society moved from one epoch to another, the basic fact of dialectic and struggle remained. Therefore, though the man of Rome differed in many respects from the man of the Middle Ages, there was between them basic continuity of type. And it is quite conceivable how some men of late Rome became men of the early feudal period, the same man moving from one epoch into the first stage of the other. So, too, the men who made the French Revolution could be the same men who acted in the hectic days which followed it because the basic pattern of history remained that of dialectic and struggle.

But the assumption which undergirds the classless society is precisely the assumption that the basic pattern of life will be changed. This is, indeed, the Marxist hope of getting rid of social evil. But this leaves the question in stark outline: How will the man formed by the pattern of history survive when the pattern of history, the dialectic and class struggle, disappears?

To escape historical evil the selves which now live and act in history would have to be destroyed. So long as the self of man is not regarded as *sui generis*, that is, a particular after its own kind, but rather as derivative from the material substratum which forms it, that self must disappear if the material undergoes radical change. This means that the men who conduct the revolution, staff and support the dictatorship of the proletariat could not enter the promised land. Nor could their children, born in the context of struggle. The gulf between history and post-history is fixed, and affords no crossing. This is instructive. It means simply that man cannot save himself.

The fact that history has no real relation with the classless society in Marxist theory serves to make the Communist quite irresponsible to history as he lives and acts in it. If the categories of history do not pertain to the Marxist paradise, why should he respect them unless he finds it strategic to do so? This is the way he acts, as can be illustrated in many ways. Before we do so, we may notice why it is that Christianity takes history just as seriously as Marxism takes it lightly.

CHRISTIANITY AND HISTORY

The Christian takes life in earnest because he views life as intimately related to heaven. While Christian doctrine views man as indissolubly soul and body as he lives and acts in history, it will be easier to consider both separately for the moment. The Christian conception of heaven involves the belief that the *same* soul which "pilgrims" on earth is the soul which is received into heaven, cleansed in the blood of the Cross. What that soul does on earth affects its status in heaven, and Saint Paul speaks of a difference in glory as between one star and another, and as between sun and moon. History is significant for the soul, not only as the meeting place, so to say, of man and God, symbolized and effected in the Incarnation, but as the testing and disciplining arena in which all men run toward the goal.

Further, writes Calvin, "We shall rise again with the same bodies we have now, as to the substance, but . . . the quality will be different." As the risen body of the Savior bore still the marks of the nails, so in some sense the risen bodies which men possess when body and soul are reunited by God exhibit close connection with the bodies they knew in history. It would be speculative to draw inferences from these doctrines, but one implication is clear: history is significant. It is the seed-time of existence, and "whatsover a man soweth, that shall he also reap." For his deeds in history, each man will be judged by God, "that every one may receive the things done in his body, according to that he hath done, whether it be good or bad." To assume, therefore, that the Christian doctrines of God's election and God's providence render history meaningless is to miss one half of the paradox which was mentioned before. To suppose that Christianity does not take history seriously is to misunderstand the doctrines of the *historical* advent of Christ, His historical life, His historical death, and His historical resurrection. To deny, or to explain away the historical reality of these is to rob Christianity of its meaning, its truth, and its power. To take these earnestly, however, is to take history with deep seriousness.

In a sentence: Marxism is true to its "theology" when it takes no real account of history; Christianity is true to its theology when it takes history in sober earnest.

MARXIST UTOPIANISM AND REAL SOCIETY

If the Marxist's removal of the concept of the classless society were only a clever tactical device, designed to take it beyond criticism, then the critic might envy him his dexterity and turn to more fruitful concerns. Quite to the contrary, however, this Marxist utopianism is far more than a rhetorical device. It has telling consequences on Marxist conduct, for, as suggested above, it has the effect of freeing him of responsibility to the world in which he lives.

Though Marx and Engels derided utopianism, they nonetheless fashioned, in their vision of the classless society, a utopia of their own — with this considerable advantage, that it was beyond criticism. For, obviously, the history in which we now live is the only history we know. If its categories do not apply to the Marxist post-history, then there is no real restraint upon the dreams which the Marxist fancy may indulge. It is for this reason — that man is enmeshed in history — that Christian doctrine holds that man learns of God's way of salvation only by revelation, and for this reason the Christian cherishes a *Book* as the living Word of God.

Freed from historical restraint, there dwells in the back of each Marxist's mind his own vision of society as it should be, and as, he is persuaded, it will be. This vision is not so much specified as it is the *feeling* that man will one day achieve his own perfection. In the light of this personalized version of the millennium, or moved by this vague feeling that perfection can be won, the Marxist wields the axe of his judgment upon the society in which he lives.

It is for this reason that the Marxist, like every other type of irresponsible critic, can be so righteously vehement in his denunciation of things as they are. He always compares them, perhaps quite unconsciously, with things as he wishes them to be. He never limits himself by the circumstances, the environment, the stage of progress a project has made, the lessons of past failures or past successes, or the demands of morality. He brushes all these aside. What control has imperfection upon a man bent one way toward perfection! He operates from a free and infinitely flexible base: his own private conception of what the new society will be like, combined with his complete irresponsibility to his environment. He has the advantage of every "out" in that he can criticize without assuming responsibility either for what he criticizes, or for what he suggests. He can judge the possible in the light of the impossible, and always find it wanting.

The Marxist does not find himself obliged, as does, say, the Christian social critic, to temper his critique of society by serious reckoning with what can be accomplished by starting "where we are," and taking cognizance of imperfect man in imperfect society. By no means. The Marxist can, and does, decry, denounce, imprecate and condemn every evil and semblance of evil, every painfully wrought social achievement and hope of achievement, all in complete irresponsibility to the context in which the evil arises or the progress that has been made. Why? Because he judges the present out of a totally different context: his own version, or feeling, of what the new world will be like.

And so Marx himself could scoff at thinkers who proposed this remedy or that program for social improvement, because they were bound to the possibilities attainable within history, while Marx transcended history, in theory. He could, and did, jeer at the slow, difficult progress which sincere and dedicated men were making toward melioration of the very injustices he noted so avidly, and yet not lend one of his exceptional talents to their support. Why not? Because he dreamed of utopia, and thus loosed himself of all responsibility to history as it passed by his door. His absolutism unfitted him for limited tasks and modest but real social achievement.

So, also, Engels could title one of his books, *Socialism, Utopian and Scientific*. In it he could extol Marxism as the one "scientific" answer to man's innumerable social problems, while charging the programs of other thinkers with being visionary. All the while, of course, it was some of these "visionary" programs, including those of dedicated Christians like Ludlow, Maurice, and Kingsley, to mention only the most famous, which were making real social progress, while "scientific" Marxism dissolved every social bond it touched. Secure in the assertion that revolution and classless society were inevitable, Engels paid no heed to patching up the society in which human life was daily lived, even those very human lives he found most exploited.

Though, of course, Engels does not put it so, what he really demonstrates, and what Marxism really testifies, is that the problem of human evil is insoluble so long as men remain within the confines of history, and are, in consequence, forced to reckon seriously with its limitations. The only escape from evil, man discovers, is in God. Denying this, Engels finds his escape in a "scientifically" established revolution and utopia.

The awesome demonstration that evil is inextricably woven into the pattern of human history, which is the conclusion to which Marxism comes, led Marx and Engels to seek escape from evil outside history. And so they foisted their utopia upon the historical process, while never really implicating it in history, or deriving it from history, at all. Instead of taking to his knees, the Communist took to his dreams; and all mankind is the poorer.

The problem the Marxist has on his hands in trying to exclude the classless society from the reign of the dialectic has often been remarked. The neat slight of hand by which he seeks to keep the concept of utopia while excluding it from the range of criticism also leaves him free of obligation to the society in which he lives. Meanwhile, he is loud in his insistence that only he really takes history as normative. Only he pays scrupulous attention to the scientific investigation of history, and rests, for this reason, his system upon a far more realistic appreciation than his opponents have of historical realities. For this reason the charge most frequently levelled by Marxists against "idealists" — that is, those who take spirit as more significant than matter in human life, and therefore in history — is that these "idealists" ignore or falsify history, and weave their own philosophy out of their own imaginations. How eloquent, indeed, the Communist can grow when he declaims upon the fanciful visions in which "idealists" indulge. And how grave he can become as he asserts that only Marxists are hardheaded enough to take history as real and normative. He, the Marxist is assured, thinks "concretely." No man for abstractions is he. Marxism alone takes reality as it is. (He might pound the lectern to prove it.)

Indeed? How does the Marxist know, for example, that dialectical materialism governs human life? He replies: by a critical examination of history. Whence hath he heard that private property is the root of all evil? Out of the mouth of history. Where is Marxism demonstrated "scientifically"? In the laboratory of history.

This very historical process which is denied all implications for the Marxist conclusion (the classless society) is exalted as proving the Marxist premises. Clearly the conclusion does not rest upon the premises at all. It is the verdict of an act which the Marxist despises in theory, an act of faith, which makes Marxism, for all its denial, a religion. And which suggests what the Christian well knows, that the only hope of salvation is by faith. But *true* salvation comes only by *true* faith.

Instead of leavening society, a figure often employed to symbolize the working of Christianity in its environment, Marxist faith disintegrates society. Instead of leading its devotees to employ their often exceptional talents and vigor in slow and painful social progress, Marxist faith makes them the professional enemies of their society. They support measures for social improvement only when this support is warranted in view of revolutionary strategy.

Meanwhile the Marxist always holds the "idealists" strictly accountable for their historical position. He is quite right in this conclusion, though he does not intend it in its real significance. Taking history seriously becomes the price the anti-Marxist must pay for being anti-Marxist — and rightly. This might, indeed, be remarked as the infallible sign of the anti-Marxist: he is stuck with history, and he knows it! If he is conscious of its significance, he welcomes it!

To the Marxist, however, being stuck with history becomes, quite paradoxically, a grave defect. In pressing home the advantage he gains from unconsciously standing upon a utopian base theoretically outside history, he confines all his critics to the limitations of history in order to destroy them. The paradox of Marxist utopianism comes full circle. He who boasts his respect for history in theory, actually condemns his opponents for taking it seriously. He does it by one word. It is the one label the Marxist has for all his critics, a label which he uses as a quite devastating epithet: *bourgeois.*

Bourgeois! To be anti-Marxist is to be bourgeois. If words could destroy, that word would demolish all to whom and to which it is applied.

What does it mean? It means to the Marxist that all his opponents are *caught* in the web of history. They are inescapably blinded by their class status. So subtly does history, in the dialectic and the class struggle, mold the perspective of those who attack Marxism, that they actually imagine their anti-Marxism to be the verdict of objective investigation. In fact, however, they can no more doff their class blinders than they can understand *Das Kapital.* Bourgeois has become the Marxist imprecation. What it really means is that anti-Marxists take history seriously. If the Marxist could bring himself to admit this, he might be less doctrinaire and of more use to mankind.

The spectacles which class struggle fastens upon the eyes of all anti-Marxists do not, it appears, cling to the noses of Marxists themselves. How they manage to get rid of them, and are thus enabled to see things straight and see them whole is, on a materialist basis, a problem more easily ignored than explained. How, to change the figure, the Marxist escapes the historical labyrinth and reaches his transcendent lookout is, perhaps, a professional secret. What it means is that the Marxist not only refuses to be bound by history, but *also* refuses to be bound by his own historical materialism. If man will not acknowledge himself subordinate to God, he must seek to make all things subordinate to himself, lest his finitude cruelly mock the longing for the Infinite which God has implanted within him.

The vagaries of the "Party Line" illustrate in a concrete way the Marxist irresponsibility to history. There is no knowing on what side of an issue the Party will stand, nor how long it will remain standing there. Tomorrow the Marxists may bob up on precisely the opposite side of the political pool from the one where they splashed noisily yesterday. Consistency is consonant with responsibility: the Marxist knows nothing of either. Lenin advised flexibility of response. It meant having no fixed position. No doubt it is useful for conducting revolutions, but it is at enmity with history.

The Marxist has an interesting explanation of his dexterity with principle. Modern physics shows, he says, that the chief characteristic of matter is motion. Dialectical materialism is, thus, the philosophy of *motion,* and therefore Marxism prescribes no fixed response to any situation. If this sounds like making Marxism absurd, the reader might consult Maurice Cornforth's *Dialectical Materialism,* where, following Lenin, he makes this defense of what, to outsiders, looks like Communist opportunism. What he does not explain is, how in a world of whirling motion there has arisen this very stable body of Marxist dogma against which every "deviation" is severely measured and condemned.

Whatever the metaphysical basis, the shifts in the "Party Line" have been so widely discussed, and have been so flatly self-contradictory, that there can be no doubt of the Marxist irresponsibility to logic and to society. There is only one assurance which established society has concerning the Marxist position: it is the enemy of stability and order.

There is one more tactical advantage the Marxist reaps from his utopianism. He can hold his opponents morally responsible for all social evil, and thus justify his conscience, if it tickles him, for all his own conduct against them. The reasoning he employs is simple: if private productive property is the root of all evil, then those who defend it must assume full responsibility for all evil, including that of the Marxist. The defenders of the *status quo* become, in effect, the scapegoats upon whose shoulders can be laid the burden of evil. In their destruction, evil receives its due reward.

To the Marxist this last idea, that of due reward, is of no moral consequence. The fact that, in the Marxist's eyes, those who oppose the revolution do, in effect, take upon themselves responsibility for social evil and therefore perish deservedly, if he can destroy them, has no moral implications. It is, however, expressive of a deep reality ignored by the whole evolutionary tradition of which Marxism forms a part. That reality is that all evil requires expiation. It exacts expiation. Conscience witnesses that this is so. The mystery of death declares it. The fateful consequences which follow upon some forms of misconduct suggest it. Emerson phrased its human expression when he pointed out that each evil deed shrinks the soul "until absolute badness is absolute death." The Cross of Christ phrased its divine expression when it testified that so heinous is evil that its expiation exacts the death of the Son of God. The awful reality and the inexorable penalty of evil, which is adumbrated in countless

forms of religious exercise all over the face of the earth, is
revealed in all its awe and terror by Calvary.

The Communist practice of making their enemies bear in
suffering the burden of social evil only points, in its own way,
to the Cross. The enemies of Christ bear witness to Him in de-
fiance of their intentions.

A concrete example may illustrate and summarize the argument thus far. Everyone knows that the Communist press all
over the world bitterly denounces racial discrimination in the
United States. The background for all this vehemence cannot
be that the Communist values human dignity so highly, nor that
he is so devoted in practice to human equality. His labor camps
incarcerate their millions, his machine guns mow down pro-
testing laborers. But his press blazons to all mankind the difficulties involved in desegregating a Southern university. And
why?

Well, for the cynical Communist it is the opportunity to step
forth upon the world stage as the protector of the rights of
dusky peoples the Communist hopes to win. For the cynic in
America it is the opportunity to raise doubt and discord in
which he can then work. But what for the sincere Marxist? For
him it is the denunciation of a historical situation in the light of
that vision he carries about of a perfect society. He has a vague
notion of perfect racial equality and judges contemporary problems in its light.

And the light becomes darkness. Because if you ask him
how, in the world of today, tensions may be eased, how old
prejudice may be blunted, how friction may be gradually reduced, how progress can be assured toward racial equality, what
has he to say? Where is his program? His program is dogmatic
and doctrinaire. Classless society! His effort goes now into denunciation and complaint. He accepts no responsibility to historical
conditions as he finds them in areas of great tension.

This is not to say that the Communist as a person may not be
motivated by, and act upon, humane motives in many life situa-
tions. His personal consideration for the victims of racial
prejudice may exceed, in practice, that of many professing
Christians. He may quite honestly seek to live in the light of his
utopia as he goes about his labor to agitate and explain Marxism. But his religious faith, and his political program, and
his theoretical commitment are destructive rather than constructive, and always subject to the "Line" of the day.

As often as not the patient efforts by sincere men on both sides of the color line to develop a program for healing the wounds of racism and moving forward toward general equality are blocked and distorted by Communist interference. The blasts of the Communist press may undo the planning of many weary months. Indeed, the ultimate aim of the Communist is so to stir unrest that he sharpens tensions, even as he professes to deplore them, in order that in the resulting confusion and fear and hatred he may find fertile soil for Marxist seed.

ROUTES TO UTOPIA

If Marx's study of history had persuaded him that the world was moving inexorably to revolution, that is the only conclusion he could expect to validate. For if what happens after history, is no longer history, he can claim no historical guidance or confirmation of it.

But stripped of the idea of the classless society, Marxism is a religion without an ideal, which is sentimentalism. Then it becomes in theory what it is already for many of its cynical leadership in practice, the deliberate agitation for revolution as the shortest road to ruthless personal power. The idea of the classless society is as necessary to genuine Marxism as it is indemonstrable. It must be called "scientific" because if men learn at last that Marxism is the religion of illusion — and therefore enslaves those who give their lives to it — they might seek instead that faith which frees, and gives peace to their souls.

It would not do, of course, to pretend that Marx deliberately fashioned the notion of the classless society as a neat and plausible fraud. He was neither a deliberate charlatan nor a fool. The imprint he has made upon history is not that made by the cheap or the foolish. Marx came very close to the deep springs of human life, and he cannot be brushed aside as a conscious fabricator. He had no intention of bringing a new religion into being, nor of departing one step from the ways of strict rationality and science. Those who carry a psychoanalyst's couch about in their imaginations may see in Marx's utopia some kind of escape from the hardships he endured, but there are more normal ways of accounting for his conclusion that man can save himself. And it might be worth remembering that Marx surrendered early in life all hope of a lucrative career in order to develop his way of salvation for mankind.

Marx may have taken at least two paths to arrive at what was, for him, reasonable assurance of the likelihood of the classless society. Neither path is strictly the discovery of research into history, but both are the consistent development of initial assumptions. The first route can be traced through Marx's analysis of evil, arriving *in time* at utopia. The second can be followed through the assumptions which underlie dialectical materialism. I am not suggesting, of course, that Marx consciously followed either path in the development of his system: this is a study of Marxism, not a psychological history of Marx, and I use the phraseology of the latter only as a mode of presentation.

The first path to utopia could have been built on two assumptions, which we have already discussed: (1) that man can himself create in time the perfect society, and (2) that he can do so by removing the root cause of social evil, that is, the private ownership of the means of production.

If, as the first assumption maintains, man can indeed create a perfect social order, then he has no moral right to be satisfied with less. If perfection can be attained, it is sin to aim at less and gross sin to oppose its realization for selfish ends. If, as the second assumption holds, private property in productive means is indeed the only block on the road to social perfection, man is duty bound to remove that block as soon as and in any way he can. Those who defend this roadblock perish along with it, and rightly so, if this assumption is correct.

Persuaded of these two assumptions, Marx could feel quite justified in his denunciation of social programs which aimed at less than the complete abolition of property. The whole real moral power of Marxism finally comes to rest upon these two postulates. Were they true, Marxists had every right to decry halfway measures as enemies of perfection, as the better is often the enemy of the best. That this attitude did, in fact, deflect Marx's own energies and those of his followers away from constructive channels, and did, in fact, frequently make them avowed enemies of limited social gains, was, on Marx's grounds, the price willingly paid in homage to the larger and higher good to be achieved later.

Marx never consciously phrased his choice as one freely made against his competitors. He merely assumed that he grasped the trend of history and they did not. In the background of his thinking always hovered the necessity arising out of dialectical materialism as it comes to expression in economic relations.

History was determined in its course; he only delineated its tendency.

It will be important for what follows if we pause and remark here on the universal complaint against materialism made by those who are not materialists, namely, that no materialist lives as if he were one. Marx could not account for his choice of life, nor for his uncommon singleness of devotion to that choice, on deterministic grounds. It was an act of dedicated will. If he had accepted his own choice of materialism as a predetermined act, then he obviously would have had no right to denounce others who chose to differ with him and whose choices would also have been determined by economic necessity. Where there is no freedom, there is no point to denunciation, or to persuasion, or to argument; except that, in theory, one cannot help what he does, even when he argues. But Marx lived to the full as if he and all others were quite free, writing, speaking, shouting and defying, condemning those who fell away from him, unable to work with anyone but Engels, sorrowing for his children, loving and hating, and acting in every way as if things did not have to be exactly as they were. Thus the materialist always acts. He is, after all, human before he is a philosopher, and to be human is to be free, free even to deny freedom.

We must face, then, these two assumptions about evil as honestly as we can. Once again, they are: (1) man can achieve his own social perfection, and (2) to do so he need only destroy the private ownership of the means of production.

In assuming, first of all, that man can make his own salvation, Marx simply echoes the evolutionary optimism described earlier. It is this optimism which has taken some rude jolts in the last few years. Had Marx lived one hundred years later, now when optimism has entered the shadows, he might himself have wondered what kind of creature it is who incinerates his fellows, sets his course deliberately upon genocide, herds men, women and children into cattle cars for slow death in labor camps, drops fire bombs on women and babes, looks with some complacency on slums, and, just to shift the focus, cannot even control his speed on the highway sufficiently to avoid an accident toll which is, in America at least, a national disgrace.

About all this, and the far more subtle nuances of evil which these national and international crimes magnify and reflect, Marx has only two choices: either, first, man acts as a free agent and deliberately chooses to commit his sins; or, second, man is the victim of economic determinism and cannot do otherwise than he does.

If Marx takes the first option, as he and Engels seem sometimes to want to do, and allows that man is free to choose the evil which he does, then Marx has to account for his hope that this sort of creature will ever freely choose to leave off doing evil that good may abound. When and how will he change his stripes? Why will he? On what day will he suddenly decide to sin no more? And if then, why not now? In short, if man is free, and if man does freely choose to do evil now, how can Marx be assured that this kind of man will not choose to sin in the classless society?

Marx cannot, of course, take that first alternative and have any real hope for the classless society left. So he chooses the second, that man is not free and therefore is not responsible for the evil which he now does. But we examined at some length what happens to man's hope of entering the classless society if man is not personally responsible for the sins he commits. The conclusion was that he then is driven to greater evil, and has no assurance of his own salvation in the classless society. Further, as has just been pointed out, Marx himself cannot, and in fact did not, live within the assumption that man is *not* free. His whole life's work is meaningless unless men can freely choose to be Marxists.

In summary, man cannot be assumed to be capable of making his own salvation. The assumption counters experience and consistency both. For, if man sins freely now, there is nothing in experience to suggest that he will choose freely not to sin when the revolution is over. On the other hand, if man is determined by economic laws in all his actions, then Marxism itself is meaningless.

Now, of course Marx knows these things. But he rests his hope on the second assumption, that private property is the root of man's evil acts. It is obvious, however, that Marx can hold to this assumption *only* if he holds to the *first*, namely, that man is not free in the evil which he does and therefore can be brought by the passage of time to his own salvation. For, if man can freely choose to sin, then property is not the only possible roadblock to utopia; it is, then, man himself who chooses to sprinkle tacks on the highway. And then property is only one means among many of bringing evil as well as good to social expression. So in order to hold that property is the root of evil,

Marx must hold that man's actions are determined for him by material laws coming to expression in economic relations.

But if he holds that man's actions are determined, he is once again unable to account for Marxism. In short, he needs human freedom in order to account for his own life and to rationalize his efforts to make others into Marxists; but he needs determinism in order to call property the only cause of evil. So he takes both positions; and it is accurate, I think, to say that his assumptions contradict each other.

This charge, of course, the Marxist can freely make against Christianity, but there is this major difference: Christianity reckons with *paradox,* and as will be suggested in a moment, with *mystery,* as *constitutive* elements in *man's* grasp of the world. Marx denies these both, and has therefore no "right" to contradiction or inconsistency among his assumptions. The Christian "right" to these lies in his recognition that now he sees "through a glass darkly" and for that reason accepts in complete confidence what the Scriptures teach, awaiting the time when he "shall see face to face," and know even as he is already known. The criticism of Christian assumptions, therefore, lies in comparing them with the Bible. The criticism of Marxist assumptions lies in comparing them with each other.

What Marx does is to take one example of how evil comes to expression in human life, and makes that form of it the root of all evil. Having made this fundamental assumption, he can clearly envision the removal of evil from society when the one root of it is destroyed. To account, however, for the ubiquity of evil, in all its hideous forms, and in all its subtle intrusions into every human relationship, by *one economic relationship* is something akin to insisting that the Great Pyramid might just as easily have been built upside down, standing on its apex.

There is no law of logic to keep one from finding the cause of evil anywhere he likes, if he seeks it in his own way. Were the Marxist given to quoting Scripture, he might ingeniously exegete Saint Paul to the effect that "money" is indeed the root of *all* evil. But it is the "love" of money which Paul condemns; and a sense of proportion, as well as anthropological studies of "communal" societies, both suggest very strongly that property figures in social evil as a significant element, but not as the root of it.

So, in summary, the second assumption concerning the nature of social evil, namely, that property is its root, is neither consonant with human experience nor consistent with the freedom of action Marx exercised for himself. But assumptions long outlast criticism. They are deep-rooted in that faculty which the Marxist likes to disparage, the capacity man has for faith. The assumptions we have been criticizing rather cursorily are part of the *religion* called Communism. They survive, as they arose, because man will hope against hope, and will repeat as long as history endures the ancient heresy which was essentially the original sin, that he can live independently of God and achieve his own salvation.

The second route Marx may have taken to the concept of the classless society will be discussed in the next chapter.

CHAPTER 4

DIALECTICAL MATERIALISM

DIALECTICAL MATERIALISM, as Marx employed it, rests upon a series of related assumptions. Because it does so, it is not really involved in history, nor is it validated by history. Materialism cannot be lived as a way of life in history. It can only exist as a kind of hothouse plant alongside history. The materialist who is caught in a traffic jam honks his horn as loudly as anyone else, and expects that someone is quite free to get out of his way, if he will but choose to do so. And if the other driver doesn't move, the materialist berates him just as roundly as if that choice had been freely made. But, of course, on the assumptions of materialism, horn-honking and violent language are quite inexplicable.

Because dialectical materialism moves alongside history, as an abstract theory not involved in real life, the dialectical materialist is not obliged to take serious cognizance of history, nor responsibility to it. As a consequence of utopianism, this point has been discussed before. It is also a consequence of dialectical materialism. Despite his omnivorous study of history, Marx's system moves from its inception to its conclusion alongside history. This is the only way in which his premises could assure him of the classless society, for history does not do so.

Granted his assumptions in dialectical materialism, Karl Marx could have demonstrated the inevitability of the classless society as logically without opening one history book in the British Museum; and his conclusion would have remained as unverifiable by history if he had read every book the mighty Museum Library contains. It is Marx who came to history with a preconceived set of philosophical assumptions, and read history through them. It is Christianity which takes history seriously as it is, knowing full well that history is intimately related to eternity. Therefore, it is Marxism which divides society against itself, and it is Christianity which has inspired much of social progress since the Roman Empire. The pudding is proved by the eating, and history demonstrates the inadequacy of Marxism.

BASIC ASSUMPTIONS

The assumptions which Marx makes to take him to the class-less society by way of dialectical materialism might be outlined as follows (I do not suggest that he so outlined them for himself, but they are true, I think, to the spirit of Marxism):

(1) Matter is more real than spirit, and therefore the laws of matter dominate history.

(2) The laws of matter act dialectically, that is, the existing configuration develops its own "contradiction," and out of the struggle which ensues between them is born another pattern which retains something of both opposing forces.

(3) The laws of matter come to social expression in economic relations, which also act dialectically in reflection of the material patterns which cause and underlie them.

(4) In economics, the dialectic focuses about the means of production because these are the basic economic factors in history.

(5) The dialectic comes to expression in society in the class struggle, created by the exploitation of the many by the few who own the means of production.

(6) The whole pattern of social life, including all social evil, follows from the class struggle, or the relations of production and exchange.

(7) Changes in the pattern of social life follow upon and are caused by changes in the pattern of economic relations which, in their turn, are caused by changes in the pattern of material forces.

(8) As inevitable shifts, occasioned by the dialectic, in the pattern of material forces bring about changes in economic relations, the whole structure of society will change.

(9) When these reflected social changes include the destruction of the private ownership of the means of production, the dialectic will cease in history, class struggle will be done away, and evil will be no more.

(10) Dialectical materialism, therefore, guarantees the social salvation of mankind and the rise of the classless society to reflect the harmony which the cessation of the dialectical movement has introduced into the world of matter.

FREEDOM, NECESSITY, AND MYSTERY

It would be beyond the scope of this volume even to attempt a discussion of each of these steps. Materialism is an ancient, time-honored and time-worn doctrine. Its basic assumption that matter is more real than spirit has to be taken at face value if it is to be taken at all. If it could be validated by inference, then the question would arise at once whether the power of reason were not superior to matter at this crucial juncture of proof. Matter cannot be the ultimate category of interpretation, and also be demonstrated to be that category in terms of another. Once the initial materialist assumption has been made, many lines of reasoning will seem to support and verify it. But it remains an assumption.

Materialism is attractive to those who deny the idea of *mystery*. Just as the Marxist cannot accept paradox, that is, the humanly illogical, so also he cannot accept the idea of mystery, that is, the humanly inexplicable. This is why he is determined to explain freedom, and in so doing explains it away. The Marxist can account for all human conduct except his own. How he succeeds in transcending history if history is altogether determined by material forces is a mystery he chooses to ignore. I have suggested before that materialism cannot really be lived. It is instructive to note the difficulties the Marxist has in trying to assert that it can be.

Marx defined human freedom as consisting in the foreknowledge of necessity. Man becomes free when he recognizes that the revolution is inevitable, and then puts his energies into promoting it. This, again, is an interesting echo of Christian doctrine.

The Christian idea of freedom has two aspects: first, the Christian holds that true freedom consists in the recognition that God controls history and has a plan for it, including a moral law for man's conduct. Second, the Christian holds that man finds freedom from enslavement to his passions, fears, and longings when he recognizes and explicitly accepts that revealed will of God as normative for himself and seeks to live according to it. The Christian then comes to see that freedom is, like property, never an end in itself, but that freedom is realized only in the service of God and neighbor. The fruit of such service he finds to be joy and peace, which witness to his spirit that this understanding of freedom is in truth what freedom is. At the heart of this concept of freedom is the Christian idea of mystery. Freedom cannot ultimately be explained; it must be lived.

It is in the living that a man comes to know the truth of the doctrine. "Taste and see" is the "experimental logic" of Christianity. Both the "taste" and the "see" are equally important. The sectarians who rely only upon "taste" and have no real control of the vagaries of the imagination, and have denied that the "see" places any intellectual or doctrinal restraint upon the "inner light" have never represented the central tradition of the Christian faith. Christian *doctrine* is real and substantial and *disciplinary*. But because the *act* of freedom is a mystery, it can be understood only after it has been exercised. "If any man will do his [God's] will, he shall know of the doctrine, whether it be of God, or whether I speak of myself," said Jesus. And, once more, "If a man love me, he will keep my words; and my Father will love him, and we will come unto him, and make our abode with him." *Act,* and *then know. Seek* and *then find.*

In his *Revelation and the Modern World,* L. S. Thornton suggests that the difference between the Christian and the ordinary conception of *mystery* is this: that in Christianity mystery is explanatory when grasped in relation to life; in common parlance mystery is the hidden and recondite, puzzling and frightening. It has been the witness of the ages that Christians have come into possession of a knowledge so secure that neither the deadening monotony of daily life, nor the deadly power of persecution could shake their conviction. "I know . . ." echoes through history. Mystery is the trembling echo of joy!

Essentially, Marxism has no place for mystery, because mystery is conceived as an intellectual problem only. In consequence, the closer the Marxist seems to come to explaining freedom, the closer he seems to come to having no freedom to explain. Thus, when the Marxist formally parallels Christian doctrine by defining freedom as the knowledge of necessity, he gets into practical difficulties. In Marxism, freedom consists in the intellectual recognition of necessity, and therefore involves no choice of obedience. There can, therefore, be no real morality in Marxism and no genuine sense of responsibility. Man is not an agent, acting in his own right, but man is a fleck of foam on the whirling waves of matter. That "with the mind I myself serve the law of God," which is the final citadel of freedom which persecution cannot storm (though Mr. Gabriel Marcel points to the threat which "brain-washing" seems to pose even to this) is meaningless phraseology to Marxism.

Thus, too, the Marxist bends, not to the will of another Person, but to the blind necessity of the sub-personal. And, therefore, in the surrender of his will he does not find himself again in the answering love of accepted obedience, but he extinguishes himself as a personality. The true Party member therefore ceases to have a will of his own; he has surrendered it in the recognition of necessity. In Christianity, self-realization comes through the free choice of self-denial, in willing obedience to God's revealed commands; in Marxism, subordination to the dictate of the Party, which alone knows the path necessity follows, converts the member into a cipher, the kind of cipher which obediently confesses to crimes which lead to its execution, if need be. Nor is this martyrdom, for the free choice which would make it so has always been denied.

MAN AND NECESSITY

Marx recognized that blind necessity made Marxism meaningless. Man, he agreed, could "make his own history" but "within limits." If this does not become a tactical device, applied only when the materialist finds it convenient to employ the concept of limited freedom, then it becomes a philosophical problem of first rank. In an absolute system, any exception could become the rule and the absolutism be completely undone. If there is limited freedom, the philosophy of determinism has been breached; and even if the hole in the dyke is, seemingly, a tiny one, no human finger can so plug it as to keep the whole sea of opposing philosophies from pouring through.

Marx cannot otherwise explain, however, the fact that both he and Engels arose from, and *escaped,* the class of the bourgeoisie. To have done so is really to have stepped out of history, and out of the dialectic altogether. Now, Marx stressed that the leadership of the proletariat would indeed come from renegade bourgeoisie. He explained it on the ground that those who pitied the exploited and learned the cause of their misery could only help. But the force of pity and the power of knowledge both are difficult, if not impossible, to account for on deterministic ground. That, as a matter of fact, Marx and Engels did break from their backgrounds, and that members of the "bourgeoisie" do often expend themselves in the service of those less fortunate is patent to all. But that these things can occur in a world inexorably governed by class struggle and the laws of dialectical materialism requires explanation which the Marxist cannot provide.

No one more than Lenin illustrates the inability of the Marxist to account for himself on materialist assumptions. In his brilliant *History of the Russian Revolution,* Leon Trotsky nods at the "problem" of Lenin from various angles, and one is disposed to suspect that it troubled him.

Lenin arrived in Russia in April, leaving the train which the Germans had accorded safe transit from Switzerland to Petrograd on April 3, 1917. He set himself at once, on that very evening, in stark opposition to the course every Bolshevik was then taking. Those who heard his first speech felt as if struck on the face with a flail. In essence, he recognized, as they did not, that Russia might be driven to the proletarian revolution *before* and *without* passing through the stage of parliamentary democracy, though this was the accepted doctrine of all leading Marxists. Lenin broke through the theory, and found himself entirely alone and at odds with every leader of the February revolution. At first he seemed defeated. He did not have then, of course, the stature in the Marxist camp which he later made for himself. Only by sheer force of will and indomitable determination to guide the revolution according to his insight did Lenin at last succeed in gaining support, the most powerful being that of Trotsky himself, and going on to triumph.

Trotsky could hardly escape the significance of this act of human will in the face of historical forces. He avoids its implications by suggesting that Lenin was the only one, except, very likely, Trotsky himself, who grasped the direction of dialectical movement at the time. But Trotsky never tries to explain how any man rises above the dialectical movement to grasp it, or why Marxism in the persons of the "Old Bolsheviks" had so far missed the tide of events. Faced with the task of accounting for two kinds of Marxism, Trotsky accounts in his own way for the winner, and leaves the others to fend for themselves.

But he must have pondered on what it was that the closed train bore from Switzerland into Russia on that fateful trip the Germans so carefully arranged to take Russia out of the war. What would the revolution have been like *if* some German general had stopped that train, or *if* a stray shell had destroyed it . . . ? Did the sealed coach bring a man who was himself but the victim of his historical position, or did it bring a man whose head carried a plan which he forced upon the moving forces of history to conform them to his dominion? Did the Bolshevik revolution come as much in the mind and will of a little man of genius as it came borne on the backs of the workers and peasants whose energies the genius guided toward *his own preconceived ends?*

The phraseology Trotsky chooses in volume three of his *History* to point up Lenin's role in the revolution is arresting: "Besides the factories, barracks, villages, the front and the soviets, the revolution had another laboratory: the brain of Lenin." The language is not only arresting, but for one of Trotsky's forthrightness, instructively evasive — the problem bothers him. He is obliged to want it both ways, you will notice: a "brain" (as other materialists quickly point out — see below) is a material thing, subject presumably to matter's laws. So Trotsky carefully avoids "mind" of Lenin, and speaks circumspectly of his "brain."

Ah, but what a brain, with what laws, and what influence! To mimic Mr. Churchill: Some brain! Some laboratory! It may be, as long ago Cabanis had said, that this brain too "secreted thought as the liver does bile." But what thought, then! And thought's the thing, after all! Was it that material brain that molded history to its imperious bidding? or was it thought formed in the *mind* of a genius? Does Trotsky really hope to allay his suspicions with a choice of terminology? For he had gone at the "problem" of Lenin before, and halted then, too, with a term:

"It remains to ask," he writes in volume one of his *History,* "and this is no unimportant question, although easier to ask than answer: How would the revolution have developed if Lenin had not reached Russia in April 1917? If our exposition demonstrates and proves anything at all, we hope it proves that Lenin was not a demiurge of the revolutionary forces. But he was a great link in that chain. The dictatorship of the proletariat was to be inferred from the whole situation, but it had still to be established. It could not be established without a party. The party could fulfill its mission only after understanding it. For that Lenin was needed . . . . Lenin's arrival merely hastened the process. His personal influence shortened the crisis. Is it possible, however, to say confidently that the party without him would have found its road? We would by no means make bold to say that . . . . Dialectic materialism at any rate has nothing in common with fatalism."

But is not this precisely the question: how can dialectical materialism have nothing in common with *fatalism,* and yet remain dialectical materialism? The denial does not solve but only emphasizes the problem.

In his *Diary in Exile,* Trotsky attacks the enigma again, and is more explicit than before: "Had I not been present in 1917 in Petersburg, the October Revolution would still have taken place — *on the condition that Lenin was present and in command* [emphasis his]. Had neither Lenin nor I been present in St. Petersburg, there would have been no October Revolution: the leadership of the Bolshevik Party would have prevented it from occurring — of this I have not the slightest doubt."

What does he say here? A *man* is not only indispensable to the success of the material forces theoretically only reflected in him, but other men could have countermanded these forces! The real struggle, obviously, was not at all in the realm of subterranean powers, but in the bitter contest between human wills, a struggle motivated by diametrically differing conceptions of the meaning of events, and guided by opposing visions of the opportunities these events afforded.

Now, it is possible so to refine materialist doctrine as to account, no doubt, for the role of Lenin by interpreting his *brain* — and those of his opponents — as a material module of exceptional delicacy, so absorbing and concentrating and refracting the web of material forces that his ideas, will, and guiding objectives were truly reflections of these configurations of matter in dialectical motion. It is possible. It has been done. This interpretation itself, then, requires an explanation also (what, on these grounds, *is* explanation?) but it cannot be refuted. A materialism, however, so refined becomes in effect only a pseudo-scientific apology for phenomena which remain nonetheless mysterious — as mysterious, for example, as the great genius of Trotsky himself and his lifelong respect for ideas and ideals and his devotion to duty.

That forces are in motion in history, embedded in men, institutions, classes, events; that Lenin and Trotsky grasped with uncanny precision and breadth the lineaments of these forces in Russia of 1917 — of all this there can be little doubt. The fact of the Soviet State testifies indubitably to this. But that the roles of these men of genius, vision, ideals — and their dogged and unremitting pursuit of these ideals — should be reduced to material motion is "ideocracy" — the tyranny of a monism extended far beyond its power to explain.

There is rather another testimony here: Trotsky, like Marx before him, would bow before some power, would not claim independent right to his great gifts, would attribute the genius of Lenin to sources beyond him. Why, oh God, would he not raise thanks to Thee?

Materialists are not, of course, blind to these problems. Rudolph Schlesinger, in his *Marx, His Time and Ours,* is at some pains to answer critics who assert that Marxism cannot account, on materialist grounds, for the power which ideas and ideals do exert on human conduct, and thus on history. Marx, Schlesinger says, took full account of the influence of ideas on human history. He does not add at this point, but it is common knowledge which he can presuppose, that Engels wrote in a now famous letter that in the heat of argument Marx and he overstressed the absolute influence of determinism on human conduct. The point at issue, Schlesinger says, is where do ideas themselves come from? He answers that ideas arise, as Marx taught, from the material substratum of human life.

This answer does not so much solve the problem of the power of ideas in life, in relation to man's freedom to choose or reject among them, as simply to drive it into another context. So long as the Marxist insists that the rise of ideas and man's choice of one over the other can be explained by cause and effect, he will end in the ultimate denial of that freedom no matter on what level he conducts his investigation. The fact of mystery in human life, far from obscuring the interpretation of experience, makes, as Dr. Thornton pointed out, experience meaningful at precisely those points where life somehow evades the grasp of propositional logic. James Martineau put it in somewhat another way, but with the same intent, when he argued in his *Study of Religion* that man *knows* what freedom is only because he *is* free; just as, Dr. Martineau continued, man knows what *causality* is because he himself *acts*. Such reasoning earned Martineau the appellation "dear old duffer" from William James, but it conveys a deep truth, upon which no one acted more vigorously than James himself.

Thus at whatever level the discussion reaches, the Marxist concludes by insisting that ideal and idea can only be "explained" in material terms, if not now, then surely when science has more exhaustively studied the relation of mind to matter.

Given time enough the light of reason will surely snuff itself out.

The choice in the long run, which some men make in practice long before they come to recognize it in theory, is between the Christian sense of mystery, which is explanatory, and the determinist science, which does not so much solve the problem of choice (and the logically inexplicable which it involves) as it denies its relevance or existence.

This kind of appeal to the inability of the determinist to account for himself is age-old and well-nigh fruitless. It only provokes a counterattack upon human freedom and the ultimacy of spiritual forces which seeks to involve these in similar contradiction. One might point to the heroic sacrifice of life which Communism itself inspires, and ask if it can be explained on materialist grounds. To the materialist it can. One might point to the human hunger for the eternal, and ask if materialism can explain it. To the materialist it can.

One might point out that if capitalism is the *necessary* consequence of historical process, and if exploitation is inevitable under capitalism, as Marx maintained, why *complain* that things are thus and not otherwise? If men are, basically, matter, they should expect to be governed by the laws of matter. If these laws lead to social relations which may be described by the word "exploitation," the word itself should be ruled out as carrying connotations which do not apply to matter at all. Shall the clay turn upon the inexorable potter and complain? If Marx had complaint to make, let it be against the intrusion into a determined universe of such spiritual qualities as feelings, emotions, conscience; and of such terms as justice, love, hatred, and slavery. Let the *Communist Manifesto* itself be purged of those flaming exhortations to union and action. For by following its injunctions to the end, Marx thought man would make not "a little" of his own history, but he would make it all anew.

"There is more in heaven and earth . . . than is dreamed of" in Marxist philosophy. The hunger of the soul for God will not be satisfied with less. It is the plain lesson of Marxism in theory as well as in practice that man cannot live by bread alone. The Marxist's blindness to this plain meaning is in itself, from the Christian point of view, a tribute to the power which faith exercises over life, even when that faith is fastened upon the false god of materialism. For as it is by faith of one kind that a man is saved, it is by faith of another kind that he is lost.

GOD AND SATAN

What agency provides and directs the immense power which Marxism has exerted in recent history? What energies does Marxism tap? It is legitimately called a religion of hate? And if so, does its orientation lie toward the demonic?

The problem of *power* is complex and has fascinated man for ages. The forces unleashed in various mechanical contrivances, including now the awesome energy released by nuclear fission, bear witness to the vigor resident in the universe. The seeming prodigal expenditures of energy in solar eruptions and in the endless expanse of flaming stars declare the immeasurable and incomprehensible *power* coming to visible expression in creation.

Power likewise comes to expression in history. Not only do natural forces, both harnessed and unharnessed, exert immeasurable force in history (so much so that Marxist materialism makes this power the controlling force in history) but so also do human forces. Food becomes metamorphosed into human energy, and energy underlies human activity. Moreover, the amount of energy the human being can convert into historical consequences seems intimately governed by the mystery of the human will, in a way that materialism, as I have been arguing, cannot adequately explain. One man eats a steak — and takes a nap on it. Another eats a steak — and climbs a mountain on it. A third may eat but a crust — and evolves an idea which guides the acts of millions. The ideal, the aspiration, the intention attract the will and free great volumes of human energy.

Though power and its exercise is more taken for granted than understood, the problems it presents so far are simply intellectual. When power, under the control of a moral agent, is turned to evil, then other complexities arise. If, for example, it is believed that the universe is under the absolute control of God, then the earthquake and the storm which harm and destroy property and lives become moral problems. It is not only an intellectual question of *how*, but also a moral question of *why* power was so exercised. So again, when man himself turns his energies to do evil, moral perplexity rises as to the source and the direction of that display of power. Such questions are ancient, as I have suggested before, and are at best approached through "a glass darkly."

Christianity recognizes an alien power in the world that seeks to take direction of human will and human life. Against this power is waged man's daily moral struggle. "For we wrestle not," writes Paul, "against flesh and blood, but against principalities, against powers, against the rulers of the darkness of this world, against spiritual wickedness in high places."

This alien power is personified in a real devil, Satan, and all his minions. Opposed to this power in all its cunning, against which man alone struggles in vain, is the power of God. Reformed theology stresses that the power of God in the world acts in a general way to restrain the power of Satan, and to provide all men with sufficient strength to erect civilization and to pursue culture. Essentially depraved, which means unable to please God in his own strength, even in the culture he achieves, man has access to the redeeming grace of God in Jesus Christ. Man can draw upon this power only after he comes to the full recognition that by himself he is powerless and empty. Then the power of God can flow through him, and it is no longer he that lives, "but Christ who liveth" in him.

And so Saint Paul preached hope, resting it on the triumphant *power* of God over Satan openly demonstrated in Christ's resurrection. It is the lesson of the Cross that man must empty himself, and the lesson of the resurrection that so shall he be made full. These lessons, not understood, have made Christianity a "stumbling block" to some and "foolishness" to others, but "unto them which are called . . . the power of God. . . ."

On the basis of this same triumphant power Saint Paul also preached that men should perform in their daily lives — thus molding history — all of the virtues of charity. This they must do, not out of human energy, but out of man's capacities infused, purified, disciplined and empowered by the Spirit of God. Christianity through the ages has never required of a man that he live in love and that he steward his talents and his possessions *in his own resolution*. It has offered him freely the *power* with the injunction.

I recite this common Christian knowledge as preliminary to the question of the source of the tremendous energy which Communism releases into history. The fact is that this power has been disruptive, destructive, and negative in its historical impact, except for the technological and material advances made in Russia and Central Europe. Its only justification for all this negation is, as I have tried to show, the promise of a utopia after the storm. This promise is, I have tried to show, illusory. The Marxist has, however, the defense that in time all will be well. Time is the bank upon which he draws his ultimately worthless checks; but so long as time endures, the doors of the bank remain open for business.

The wheat and the tares, Christianity teaches, grow up together until that time when the Divine Reaper gathers into His barns the grain and gives the weeds over to destruction. It is not revealed to those growing in the field of history what the final harvesting will be. The testimony of Saint Paul is the witness of all the saints: "Oh, wretched man that I am. . . ." This knowledge of the ambiguity in his own life chastens and subdues the tendency one might have to render offhand judgment on others. No doubt Communism has released vast amounts of demonic fury into history, and no doubt many Communists have little cared that this is so. Deceit, torture, murder, hatred and varied sorts of crime are not the fruits by which a tree rooted in love is known. No doubt, also, as Dr. Maritain has maintained, the doctrines of Communism not only express atheism but presuppose it. Many Christians have seen in the scourge of the Communist whip God's judgment upon the sins of men in the world of economics. It is the sound advice of Calvin that in such a time of persecution, those who understand it as the hand of God look to their own sins rather than denounce those of others.

THE POWER OF NEGATION

What concerns the philosophy of materialism in all this, however, is the use which the Communist, like Hegel, deliberately makes of the concept of *negation*. One need not speculate here on the theoretical and actual power of the demonic, but simply take cognizance of the metaphysical status which Communism accords to the *negative* in life and in history.

The problem of sin in Christian theology becomes the problem of negation in philosophy. The question is: what measure of reality must be accorded to evil? Augustine, and those influenced by him, regarded evil metaphysically as the absence of good, or the privation of being, or, as negation. Perhaps under the influence of Platonism, Augustine thought of evil as derivative, as perverted or misdirected good, surviving parasitically on the existence of the good and having no ontological reality in itself. Sin was thought of as missing the mark, being less than one should, the absence of virtue, power spent amiss. The power of the devil is, then, the power to direct man's energies away from God, while those energies themselves arise out of the only source of energy in the universe, God Himself.

Now, Marxist thinkers rest their philosophy frankly upon the *reality* of negation, opposition, the "positive" force of the contradiction. Reading history and the reality which is presumed to underlie it through Hegelian lenses, the Marxists regard each positive force as raising up a negative force which contradicts it. Out of this opposition of two *real* forces comes a "synthesis" which absorbs *something of each,* and starts the process all over again. What is to be noted is that the synthesis consists of something of *both* the forces which created it. Thus the Marxist regards negation, not as the absence of reality, but as having reality in its own right.

For example, at the level of history, where materialist metaphysics is reflected in social behavior (according to Marxism), both Marx and Engels consider the bourgeoisie as the historic embodiment of negative forces coming to expression in oppression and exploitation. Yet they are lavish in their praise of the contributions to historic progress made by this same bourgeoisie in their revolutionary destruction of feudalism. The bourgeoisie embody, so to speak, the "positive" power of the negative. It is, indeed, upon this power of the negative that history rides forward in Marx's philosophy of history. It is this fact which has given rise to calling Marxism a "religion of hate," for it is that essentially negative emotion which releases much of Marxist enthusiasm and power. It must be remembered in passing, however, that much of that hatred, which Dr. Maritain calls "resentment," has been provoked by the profound failure of Christians to live up to their profession in social, particularly economic, life,

In like manner, the power of negation in Marxist thought is reflected in the role Marx assigns to the proletariat. It is the function of the proletariat, finally, to bring in the new society by the destruction of the bourgeoisie. It is negation which carries progress in its bosom, in Marxism, and plays in history a positive part. Yet, its effect in the historic process is, as might be anticipated, always destructive. Metaphysically, as well as historically, the Marxist has no positive agent which carries the reality of the classless society within itself. And this is why, viewed metaphysically, the classless society cannot be achieved. This is why, also, the Marxist is ultimately irresponsible to history; no reality binds him.

It is this kind of metaphysic which assures the Marxist that out of the terrors of the dictatorship of the proletariat, a *good*, that is positive, society may eventually come. For it must be remembered that the classless society is not supposed to follow immediately upon the revolution, even if that were considered a positive achievement. One last negation — the ruthless extermination of the last remnants of capitalism — will still follow, and *out of this negation*, indeed *upon its back*, the good society is presumed to arrive. Good does not arise out of evil, in Marxism, because (as in Christianity) the good has been there all the while, but enslaved and perverted. Good, in Marxism, arises out of the "positive" force of evil itself. The negative gives birth to the positive. The grotesque offspring of such a parent is visible in Communism the world over.

This is the moral consequence of dialectical materialism. It is the inevitable result of taking negative forces as real and as possible bearers of real good. Nor is this an accident in Marxist thought. Lenin stressed the value of the dialectical negation, and many Marxist thinkers have praised the insight into history which the Marxist dialectical metaphysics affords.

The Christian doctrine that evil is overcome only by good has given rise to the Christian metaphysic which regards, as did Augustine, evil as parasitically borne on the power of good. Evil thus has reality, but always a derivative reality. Sin is desperately real, but yet does not exist in its own right. Freed from the distortion of evil, the good may once more act in its own capacity in life and through life. This freedom is achieved in the Christian's life by his appropriation through faith of the liberating power of God.

It is true that many Christians often, and all Christians at times, have acted as if good might arise out of the active employment of evil. The conspicuous examples are the Inquisition and Protestant counter-persecutions. Less conspicuous examples occur every day. But the distinction between the Christian and the Communist metaphysics is clear and decided: the Christian rejects, while the Communist embraces, the ultimate reality of negation. As a consequence, when the Christian has been true to *his* faith, he has been a positive force in history; and where the Communist has been true to *his* faith, he has been a destructive force in history. In life, where consistency and inconsistency intertwine, some Christians have laid about them with a heavy hand; and some Communists have, as Mr. Chambers recounts so vividly in the introduction to *Witness,* given their lives for their fellows in heroic self-denial.

CONCLUDING CRITIQUE

The discussion of the underlying assumptions of dialectical materialism may be concluded with a series of observations:

(1) The attempt to make meaningful the concept of "dialectic" in its application to the realm of matter depends, really, upon looking at matter through the eyes of mind. The assumption that matter, which Marx and the later Marxists think of in terms of forces in movement, acts dialectically is not validated by a study of atomic physics. Dialectic is, rather, interpreting movement in matter as following the pattern of observable movement in society, and applying terms to it which have applicability only to mental processes. A mental contradiction is understandable; the tension and opposition between physical forces is also understandable; but to suppose that these physical tensions arise by *self*-contradiction, and are resolved when some third force arises which absorbs something real from each of the competing forces is the gratuitous imposition upon physics of concepts which take real and meaningful significance only in mind. But, if this is true, Marxism makes mental categories superior to matter, which is fatal to materialism.

(2) A second observation is that Marx has often been criticized for simply asserting that the dialectic will cease in the classless society. This assumption rests again upon reading matter through spectacles provided by other forms of reality. It is understandable how, if classes could be united, or if one of two opposing classes could be totally destroyed, there would be, theoretically, no further class struggle. The idea is clear, even if impossible of actualization. It seems likely that it is this imagined concept which leads Marx to assert that the dialectic will no longer work in matter in the new era. But, obviously, this is an inference *to* matter *from* society. Materialism, in principle, always derives society *from* matter. Marx is again involved in the practical denial of what he theoretically defends. But he has no other ground for asserting that after the revolution the dialectic at the level of matter will cease. He can only assert this on the supposition that the course of the dialectic has achieved its goal; something which matter, presumably, knows or cares nothing about.

(3) There is, in life and in thought, that subtle inversion of the affirmation into its opposite which is also called the "dialectic." It is their insistence upon it which has earned for Professors Barth and Brunner and their school the title of "dialectical theologians." It may be illustrated by our own argument that under public ownership of productive means *all* of the people own them, and therefore *none* (no one) of the people own them. Lenin is supposed to have slapped his knee one day and exclaimed that now he saw the dialectic at work, too, when some such paradox came to his attention. But this form of the dialectic is a long way from dialectical materialism. And it is simply by assumption that Marx reads into matter this subtle turning-upon-itself which Hegel recognized as characteristic of thought, or of spirit. Here, as in materialism itself, the Marxist takes one aspect of experience and elevates it to the position of determining the whole.

(4) There is, also, struggle in life. It is possible, too, to view society as divided into classes. But, as the experience of Marxism in action clearly shows, struggle intrudes within as well as between groups. Indeed, the most basic form of struggle a man knows is within himself, even the man who recognizes no moral demands but has to choose which pleasure to take and which to postpone. The lines of struggle cross and criss-cross in any society at so many angles that it is oversimplification of the highest order to view society as made up of classes locked in deadly and inescapable struggle. While the Marxist recognizes it to be one of the duties of Marxism to make clear to the proletariat that, in reality, this confused pattern of struggle revolves about one essential conflict, nevertheless the fact that Marx could avoid struggle with no one, even Engels, has been but the beginning of the Marxist inability to keep the pattern of struggle clear even within the Party itself. Struggle is real enough. But *class* struggle is doctrinaire and far from an exact analysis of social behavior.

(5) Finally, the charge with which we began our discussion of this second route which Marx may have taken to his conception of utopia was that in reality dialectical materialism is a way of approaching history and not a verdict of its scientific study. This philosophical position exists alongside history, but is not validated by it. The Marxist does not himself live it; human freedom denies it; and the metaphysics of dialecticism demon-

strate at best that negation taken seriously has disruptive effects upon history.

To the Marxist the ever-living voice pleads still that he take off his blinders, remove those filters which sinisterly absorb much of the light of his own experience, and that he lift up his eyes unto those hills from whence real help cometh, and with us all accept the invitation from Him who calls still, "Come unto me all ye. . . ."

CHAPTER 5

LIBERALISM, MARXISM AND CHRISTIANITY

RIVERS OF INK have cascaded down from immense glaciers of learning and swept through every tributary of Marx's economic theory. The few modest drops I might add to the torrent will not affect the stream at all, but will complete the discussion of Marxism for this volume. Labor value, surplus value, class struggle, the economic basis of society, and every other Marxist tenet have each excited vigorous controversy, and the library shelves groan under the many volumes which embalm once heated words.

CONTEMPORARY CAPITALISM

One question each critic of Marxism must face is whether the Marxist analysis of capitalism as bound for inevitable disaster is sound. Perhaps the best answer is not theoretical so much as practical: we should look soberly about us. As we do, it is well that we bear two injunctions in mind:

(1) Life does not fit neat theoretical categories. Any generalization like "labor value," or "surplus value" sums up certain aspects of experience, and omits others. Illustrations can always be brought against whatever general position one takes regarding social phenomena. This is the basis for much altercation between various economic theories. One must rest, therefore, on what seems to him the best interpretation, without expecting to be invulnerable to attack.

(2) We live among imperfect men, being ourselves imperfect, and in an imperfect world. This fact can be made the excuse for letting evil abound and allowing the devil to take the hindmost without doing much about it. So to employ the fact of sin is, from the Christian point of view, sin itself; and from any ethical point of view, slothful inhumanity. On the other hand, this does mean that the imperfect can only *approach* per-

fection, but never achieve it. It is, we must remember, a Marxist trick to judge society *as if* it could be perfect. If man does not seek to move toward perfection, he fails of his duty; if he demands perfection or nothing, he fails altogether. One element which must always figure in our social judgments is the "human predicament." Man sins.

It is for this reason that Calvin advocated political democracy, that the sins which governors, like all other men, are prone to commit, might be under the control of those who suffer by them. It is for this reason, I have suggested, that capitalism, with all the faults of which critics are aware, offers the best organization for the satisfaction of economic needs; because it is flexible enough to allow correction of fault and error.

And so, to answer the question: was Marx right about the destiny of capitalism, we need but look soberly about us. The answer is obviously, No, though the Marxist would say, Not yet!

As compared with what Marx knew, and predicted, are conditions of labor better, or worse? Are economic goods more widely distributed, or less? Is there more leisure, or less? More gross exploitation, or less? In short, has the law of the "increasing misery of the proletariat" been verified, or broken?

The answers to all of these questions point indisputably in one direction: Western society has made gigantic strides away from the grim days Marx knew. Capitalism has provided, and does provide, a far higher economic level for far more persons, within a far wider range of personal freedom, than Marx supposed possible. The Christian who does not recognize this, and thank God for the opportunity it affords for further constructive development, blinds himself to the moral significance of the fact that Marx, brilliant analyst that he was, went so far wrong.

Communists recognize that Marx's predictions, which were already proving false during his later life, have not been fulfilled. Marxist criticism has been obliged, therefore, to shift from seeking out naked exploitation, which no longer has a typical appeal, to attacking crises and depression. These very real threats to the stability of Western society present a massive challenge to the *moral* and *intellectual* ingenuity of capitalism.

The Marxist is still persuaded that capitalism is doomed. He argues that its successes have been the result of a ruthless exploitation of natural resources, coupled with technological achievements which Marx could not envision. So long as this explanation is not employed to explain away the real achievement of economic distribution, it contains much truth. What it ignores, however, is that moral and religious demands have come to exert influence in the market-place in a way that Marx did not envision. These demands and their "interference" in the market have played their part in blunting the force of the evils Marx described. Capitalism has not gone the way which Marx laid out for it, in large measure because it has not gone the way which classical economics laid out for it. And the Marxist contention that capitalism, though taking a path by way of far higher general prosperity than Marx supposed possible, is nonetheless on the road to destruction, will be ultimately defeated by continued "intrusion" into the realm of economics of Christian moral considerations.

Whatever, for example, may be the economic truth about "labor value" (that labor contributes the only real value to a commodity) the theory itself arose long before Marx, and it embodies the universal recognition that labor is creative because it is a man's gift of himself. This means that the exercise and control of labor at every level, from executive to part-time employee, have religious and ethical overtones. This means that the conditions under which work is performed, the dignity of the laborer, and the primacy of the human over the material values in industry are all religious as well as economic concerns. This is the truth of the theory of labor value, on a level other than that on which Marx employed it.

Again, the theory of "surplus value" (that profit comes only from exploitation) has given rise to intricate economic dispute. Marx obviously underrated the value of initiative, the worth of capital, the nature of risk, and the value of distribution services. But, apart from the economic aspects of the immensely complicated problem of the distribution of the fruits of industry, the appeal which the theory of surplus value has made lies in the common recognition that the rewards of labor must be *fairly* distributed among those who produce them, whether they be owners, managers, or machine operators. This is the truth of the theory of surplus value on a level other than that on which Marx employed it.

Thus, in mid-twentieth century, capitalism neither acts as if it were tottering toward revolution, nor as if it were the legitimate offspring of what Marx knew as its father. The reason, in brief, is that economic laws have been modified in practice to some degree by religious and moral commands. The reason why a society ordered, as mid-nineteenth century England was ordered, solely by the laws of economics cannot escape degeneration is that economic laws are in the last analysis dictated by relations between things and man's desire for things; and therefore other human interests and higher values often perish by the wayside. Where Marx went astray was in believing that no other laws could interfere with economic laws. He took this position because he was bound by philosophical materialism to the assumption that the laws between things are the primary laws in life. The failure of his predictions is in itself *prima facie* evidence that materialism can be superseded in practice by principles arising out of spiritual forces whose highest expression is in Christianity.

As a simple matter of fact the laws of the free economy advocated by the school of Adam Smith, and commonly called the Manchester or *laissez faire* school, have been made subservient in crucial instances to the recognition of human needs, human dignity, and human moral responsibility to God and to man. Marxism has been refuted in practice in the very marketplace where it professed to find its strength because the laws of economics have been made subject to other demands whose origin is essentially Christian. But the exponents of economic liberalism must not forget that when Marx was proved a *false prophet,* Adam Smith was proved a *false theorist.* The modifications of *laissez faire* which Marx failed to take into account were at the same time corrections of the extreme position of Smith and his followers. There are those still who seem quite distressed that Marx has been made so bad a prophet by the demonstration in practice that Smith was not infallible. It is a wise child who knows his own father.

CLASSICAL LIBERALISM

And what kind of father was Adam Smith? Smith lived in that sanguine time when man was presumed to be on the open road to perfection. How might this kind of man, rational and growing morally better as days went by, best provide for his economic needs? The answer Smith gave to this question, and its development by his followers, make up what is called classical economic theory.

Man is, said Smith, a bundle of desires. He seeks their satisfaction and avoids their frustration. In consequence, each man seeks his own good, and is obliged to limit his search only by the seeking of others. The world of economics is the arena in which man seeks satisfaction of his desire for goods of all kinds. In this arena each man pursues relentlessly his own ends. And yet out of this seeming clash of myriad self-interests comes, Smith maintained, a unique harmony of interests, as though it were provided especially by an unseen guiding hand. This harmony is represented by the balance of supply and demand. This free interplay in the economic arena of what Smith called each man's "enlightened self-interest" is, he said, the key to economic progress: "enlightened" in that each does not interfere immorally with the self-seeking of others: "self-interest" in that no one considers any concerns other than those legitimately his own.

If, now, Smith's description of the economic process were correct, it is clear that any interference from any source with any part of the system would upset the delicate balance of the whole. To prevent such interference is, Smith argued, the sole function of the state. It should act to protect the two "sacred rights" of property and human life, to curb dishonesty, and to umpire disputes in the courts. The secular deity whose invisible hand guided universal selfishness into universal good must suffer no interference from state, church, or any other agency, lest he sulk and refuse to harmonize competing wills.

It is obvious that *laissez faire* (let people do as they choose) economic theory moved on several large assumptions. So long as they proved correct, the rather sublime vision which Smith and his followers beheld of *universal* happiness and prosperity bid fair to be realized. As soon, however, as any of these assumptions proved false, there would enter into economic relations a kind of interference which would destroy the balance just as effectively as the kinds of interference which Smith feared. Several of Smith's assumptions did prove false, and their falsity did upset the balance Smith envisioned, and "interference" from other sources has been necessary to redress the balance once more.

Smith's first assumption rested upon his greatest contribution to economic thought — the idea of the division of labor. Accustomed as we now are to the idea of division of labor, we no longer realize the significance of the demonstration that ten men who each do one small part of an operation will produce more items in the same time than can ten men, each of whom makes the whole item by himself. Smith's assumption was that competition in the open market would result in ever greater

production because it would drive each competitor to greater
and greater division of labor, and thus to the production for
the people at large of an ever increasing supply of goods to
satisfy ever more human need and desire. Happiness and prosperity rested, therefore, said Smith, on free competition. The
division of labor has indeed resulted in phenomenal industrial
output, especially as the hand of man has been re-enforced or
even supplanted by the machine.

Smith's second and correlative assumption was that man is
a bundle of desires whose happiness increases in direct proportion as the flow of goods increases. This assumption has been
proved by experience to have some flaws. Modern Western man
is in possession of far more goods than his forebears, but modern
man has found that goods bring care as well as happiness. He
has learned that goods do satisfy desire, and that a steadily
rising minimum of them is almost indispensable to survival in
a mechanized world, but he has also learned that satiety is not
happiness. He has yet to learn generally that goods are not ends
in themselves, but bring happiness only when enjoyed and
stewarded for spiritual ends, a task which increases in difficulty
as goods increase.

Furthermore, as Marx himself noted, specialization in industry
is, indeed, the father of vastly increased production, but it is also
the parent of deadly monotony which threatens stultification
of mind and will. The rise of the uniform culture which chilled
Henry Adams more than half a century ago, and the rise of the
mass man who moves through the pages of Ortega y Gasset's
Revolt of the Masses and the novels of Sinclair Lewis are results
of industrialism and division of labor which Smith did not
anticipate.

Marx further observed that skilled labor was progressively
replaced by less skilled labor as the elements in the productive
process were simplified. He saw that it became increasingly
appropriate to call men "hands" with all that this description
implies of subservience to the machine, of lack of intellectual
stimulus, of anonymity, and of complete severance of the workman from pride in his own achievement. Because man is more
than a bundle of desires awaiting satisfaction with an increased
supply of goods, the vast increase in industrial output satisfied
many human needs, but only at the expense of other human
demands equally if not more real. All this Marx carefully noted.

It must not be supposed that these problems raised by industrialism are solved by Marxism just because Marx recognized them. On the contrary, those aspects of the impact of industrialism upon the individual which loom largest in the modern world are social and, ultimately, religious in nature, and for this reason Marxism is peculiarly unfitted to grapple with them. It is the assumption that man is essentially but an economic animal, one whose happiness can be achieved by multiplying his possessions, which underlies Marxism as well as it underlies classical economics. Christianity rejects that assumption and stands in as much opposition to the one as it does to the other. The human problems in industry are problems which concern the Christian and the Church because they are problems which concern not only men's bodies but also their souls. Their solution depends upon bringing moral and religious considerations to bear upon essentially economic relations. In order to do this, the Christian and the Church must deny not only Karl Marx but also Adam Smith. The fact that this is being done in parts of industry is a judgment upon both Marx and Smith.

Smith's third assumption, which proved to be his weakest, was that man is not only a bundle of desires, but is also a rational creature steadily improving his moral nature. On this ground, Smith supposed that the increased supply of national goods would be distributed in relative equality among all who produced them. He argued this way: as a free rational agent, operating in a completely free market, no man would sell his labor except at conditions advantageous to himself. This meant that as the total national production increased, each participant's share would also increase in relatively direct ratio. If the workman were denied the wage he freely demanded, Smith held, he could refuse to enter the labor contract until a fair adjustment were made, and thus bring the employer to terms.

Marx, as well as many others, detected the fly in this ointment, which upset the neat blending of competing interests which Smith predicted. As a matter of fact, Marx noted, the steadily increasing flow of wealth from the national English industrial plant did not receive relatively general distribution under the policies prescribed by Adam Smith. Some got immense shares for themselves, while others got a bare subsistence or less. Why? Well, because the laborer and employer did not meet as equals in a free labor market. The contract which English law presumed that the laborer freely entered into was in fact a cruel fiction; he had no real choice because he had no real resources.

There were, in Marx's time, and for several reasons, more labor-ers than industry absorbed, and free competition among them drove down the wage levels in the fashion predicted by Ricardo. Smith's rosy estimate that a rational man in a free market would provide a general distribution of goods was shattered by countless testimonies which Marx delved out of Royal Com-mission *Reports.*

"No man," said Jeremy Bentham, a disciple of Smith's, "of ripe years and sound mind . . . ought to be hindered with a view to his own advantage from making such bargains, in the way of obtaining money, as he thinks fit." Indeed, Marx noted; and did not this lead quite directly to the British employer who confessed to a Commission that the kind of bargains he liked to make to his advantage involved always hiring mothers with dependent children, because they worked hardest lest they be sacked and their children starve? Smith's England knew some-thing of starvation. It was as logical a development of Smith's principles as would have been universal prosperity. Indeed, it was more logical when reckoning was taken of the tendency man had to slip often from the path of steadily improving morality which Smith presupposed.

We are thus led back to the problem of evil in human rela-tions. Classical economics did not take evil seriously. Because it did not do so, there arose kinds of interference with the "laws" of economics which produced results which Smith did not foresee. Classical economics led to Karl Marx.

It is significant that this is so. Karl Marx has frequently been called the last of the classical economists. What is meant is that he took over many of the basic theories of Adam Smith and his school, and worked them out to their practical conclusions. The position of Smith in theory becomes the Marxist position in practice. Marx saw with perfect clarity that a completely unre-stricted market, in which the seeking of self-interest was not always "enlightened," leads to gross exploitation as easily as to universal happiness. Based on the classical view of economic *laissez faire,* capitalism could only lead, Marx prophesied, to increasing misery for an increasing number of people.

Marx was wrong. He was wrong because Adam Smith was superseded in the market-place by considerations of humanity, of morality, of justice and of religious values.

This is not the place to attempt even a brief survey of the history of social legislation and the rise of other forces which "interfered" with the free market. But it is clear that, for example, the rise of unions, while beset with the imperfections which dog all human endeavor, has resulted in material benefits to labor, and has endowed it with a dignity and responsibility which Marx never knew. The risk that labor will now abuse the power it has acquired is one of the risks that capitalism runs, and poses a significant challenge to the leadership of the union movement, in which the individual Christian is vitally concerned.

The control by legislation of minimum wages, hours of work, the labor of women and children, and the conditions of labor are all in violation of *laissez faire* theory. But they have contributed to the national welfare in so generally recognized a way that no one seriously proposes the abolition of such controls. Likewise, unemployment insurance, old-age pensions, and the whole range of aids for the indigent affect the free labor market, but in so positive a way that they have become national institutions. Upon all these foundations rest a hopefulness and a prosperity which furnish now the strongest basis for anti-Marxist persuasion. To have escaped the laws of Smith is to have defeated the appeal of Marx.

So, again, the federal income tax has indeed interfered with the freedom of many to do as they wished with all of their earnings, but it has shared the costs of community life somewhat on the basis of ability to pay, and has controlled in a measure the unlimited concentration of monopoly and economic power.

The entrance of the state into economic life as a positive agent of the people, while always involving a threat of being carried too far, has in general so strengthened the national economy that Marxism has few to whom it can appeal today on the grounds of economic hopelessness. The further limitation of the extent to which the state will enter economic life depends first of all upon the ability of free men to conduct their own economic activities so that justice is done, the poor are sustained, and the general welfare sits as a voting member in the making of policy decisions. Free men want neither *1984* nor *Animal Farm*. The voice of the Christian and of the Christian Church can have much to do with avoiding both by insisting that the laws of God for man extend their dominion over economic relations too.

Thus it has come about that the institutions which Marx viewed as the tools of the bourgeoisie do not play the roles he wrote for them in modern American life. Education is not chained by capitalist dogma, though there be those who rattle the chains at what they consider heresy. So far have some educational institutions avoided the Marxist pattern of bourgeois domination, that instead there are those who wax apoplectic in warning that the crimson gown is not the only shade of red at Harvard. And in England, the Cambridge professorships once staffed by disciples of Adam Smith have more recently been held by Alfred Marshall and John Maynard Keynes, both critics of *laissez faire.*

Large segments of the Christian Church have so violently denounced the use of religion as a sedative, and so vigorously condemned the "pie-in-the-sky" promises of yesteryear, that some segments of orthodoxy are given to wondering if they believe in heaven at all; and some critics see a Communist conspiracy in every economic pronouncement of the National and World Councils of Churches.

Though the vast power of the state acts now in this way, and again in that, it is so far from being the "committee of the bourgeoisie" that some detect a steady trend to the left, and still others think socialism already arrived in America, while it has openly come to pass in England.

In short, whether as a result of the shift in economic forces achieved by moral control of the market, or for reasons less obviously Marxist in form, the institutions of capitalist society present to Christianity the challenge to exert ever larger influence in their development, rather than exhibiting the pattern which Karl Marx predicted they should.

CHRISTIAN SOCIAL CRITICISM

We may conclude with some hints regarding the kind of influence which Christian social criticism might more and more exert in economic life and related social institutions.

As I have suggested before, the foundation of Christian social criticism is the Word of God revealed in the Scriptures and supplemented by the laws of creation. Basic to the Christian approach to social relations is the fact of the resurrection of Christ.

Nothing in sacred nor in secular literature rises to heights rhetorically more powerful or spiritually more sublime than does Saint Paul's exposition of the meaning of the resurrection in the fifteenth chapter of First Corinthians. And his verdict is final: ". . . if the dead rise not, let us eat and drink; for tomorrow we die. . . . But now is Christ risen from the dead, and become the first-fruits of them that slept. . . . For this corruptible must put on incorruption, and this mortal must put on immortality." Each man is destined to rise from the dead. Every man faces the resurrection "and after that the judgment." In this fact resides the final authority which Christian ethics exerts upon economic relations.

There is continuity between history and eternity. The soul and body which live and act in history are the "corruptible" which must "put on incorruption" and the "mortal" which must "put on immortality." Delineation of what this astounding truth means for every act of each person's daily life is the complex interpretative task set before Christian thought. "For God shall bring every work into judgment, with every secret thing, whether it be good or whether it be evil." And Jesus' expression of it is, "But I say unto you, That every idle word that men shall speak, they shall give account thereof in the day of judgment."

What relation have my deeds, down to the very idle words which pass my lips, to my eternal destiny? is the question which Christian thought must answer clearly and concretely as preliminary to social criticism. What does God intend by not only permitting but by sustaining history?

There is a form of orthodoxy which tends to answer that man's relation to God is not really involved in time at all. Laying exclusive stress upon God's side of the paradox of predestination and free human will, these theologians find history essentially meaningless, a purposeless passage of time simply to be gotten through. Thus extremes meet, for atheism, too, attaches no real meaning to history. The indefinite prolongation of time, limited perhaps only by the thermodynamic law which bespeaks the gradual running down of the universe, offers the atheist no real explanation for history. George Eliot might wish to join the *Choir Invisible* which endures only in its echoes down time's finite corridor; but echoes, too, die away. The temporal does not furnish its own interpretation; and history for atheism, like history for extreme orthodoxy, is ultimately meaningless.

Theological liberalism moves in uneasy tension between its disbelief in the historical resurrection of Jesus and its belief in the universal fatherhood of God. Unable to make the Cross and the empty tomb theologically intelligible, Liberalism drifts into sentimentalism, and in its doctrine of universal salvation hardly escapes making history essentially meaningless, too. If all men are destined for heaven, the historical interim has little real significance, which is, I understand, a problem also observable in Barthianism.

In contrast to these attitudes toward time, and the deeds done in time, the Reformed Protestant tradition has found the meaning of history, as well as the paradox of history, adumbrated in Saint Paul's words, ". . . work out your own salvation with fear and trembling." There is a real heaven to be gained, and a real heaven to be lost by real and responsible choice made in history. There is a real Christ standing at the door of a real heart in real time and knocking for admission. He awaits a real choice to let Him in. This is one side of the paradox to which Reformed theology has ever clung. It is in history that responsible choice is made, that faith comes to the expression in works without which it is dead. It is to man in history that Christ says, "Whosoever shall confess me before men, him shall the Son of Man also confess before the angels of God: but he that denieth me before men shall be denied before the angels of God." It is to man thus historically confronted by the fearful choices upon which eternity hangs, involved as he is in finitude and incapable of meeting the demands of the spiritual law, that the mercy, patience, and loving-kindness of God become intense, historical realities. For it is to a man who falls in history that there is deep meaning to God's grace, and it is to a man who repents in history that there is realized the promise of God's readiness ever to renew His companionship.

Just as true is the other side of the paradox. "For it is God which worketh in you both to will and to do of his good pleasure." "By grace are ye saved." "And that not of yourselves: it is the gift of God: not of works, lest any man should boast."

History has meaning in the sense that man's acts have eternal significance. History has reality in the sense that it is sustained by the providence of God and directed by His will. Both aspects of the paradox must be grasped with equal tenacity, and both must be developed with equal emphasis, despite their logical incompatibility. It is Christian experience that, having sought and found his Lord, the Christian knows that all the while it was really his Lord who sought and found him.

Viewing history, then, "under the aspect of eternity," Christian social criticism judges economic relationships first of all in their effect upon the spiritual well-being of employer and employee, and only after that in their effect upon production and distribution. Or, again, the Christian insists that economic law shall be subject to Divine law.

"Thou shalt not steal" is the Christian approach to the problem of "surplus value."

"Therefore all things whatsoever ye would that men should do to you, do ye even so to them: for this is the law and the prophets," is the Christian approach to the "class struggle."

"Is not the life more than meat, and the body than raiment?" is the Christian approach to all of economics. "Seek ye first the kingdom of God, and his righteousness . . ." is the first rule in Christian economic theory.

In the light of these and countless other Scriptural injunctions, Christian doctrine insists that man's relation to his work and to the fruits of his work is ultimately significant only as it affects his relation with God. For "what doth it profit a man to gain the whole world, and lose his own soul?"

Living conditions and working conditions for men, women and children which befit a human being are significant because each human being is destined for eternity; and how and where he lives and works has genuine significance for his spiritual life. While the grace of God knows no barriers, and lives of great charity and spiritual beauty flourish without regard to economic status and social recognition, it is undeniable that heavy spiritual hardships may be theirs who suffer exploitation, poverty, or economic injustice. And equally heavy spiritual handicaps threaten those who possess uncommon wealth and power, for these may blind them to human need and the tasks of stewardship.

Exploitation is not only theft but as theft it deprives the exploited of the possessions rightfully his to employ in the development of his own body and soul. Poor work, loafed hours and shameless waste of materials is, equally, the workman's exploitation of his employer.

A CHRISTIAN SOCIAL ORDER

The fact that man's economic activities play so large a part in life, and occupy so much of his time and energy, makes it all the more imperative that Christian standards and Divine injunctions penetrate every relation in business, in trade, in industry, and in labor. It is this demand upon the world of economics which places Christian doctrine in unalterable opposition to the *laissez faire* theories of liberal economics as well as to the economic determinism of Karl Marx. Christianity has something to say to economics; neither Smith nor Marx shall stifle God's voice; but if the Christian and the Church fail to make that voice heard, theirs is the greater shame.

This does not suppose that the Christian acquires a grasp of industrial technique along with his faith, or that he can wax oracular on business methods. Christianity in economics means that under the guidance and stimulus of living Christian doctrine, taught from a vital Christian pulpit, press, and by dedicated example, more and more men and women shall join those who now seek to integrate their Christian confession and their economic lives. It means that the approach to all economic relations and problems shall emphasize first the spiritual and shall lay steady emphasis on the demands which the law of God, as revealed in God's revelation, makes upon the conduct of all men everywhere, at work or at leisure. It means that so long as one institution has not felt the spiritual pressure of the demands of Christ, that institution presents a challenge to Christians within and without. It means to take seriously the demand of Christ that all things shall be subjected unto Him.

It is at this juncture, as I have hinted before, that Christian education assumes a highly significant role in national life. A Christian social order must, before it can come into being, first of all receive definition. It must have a pattern, goals, and dynamic of its own. If the reader will now pause to ask himself if the *outlines* of a Christian society are well known — among Christians — and if he will also inquire if high school and college textbooks are oriented to such an outline, and if he will ask whether Christian classroom teaching has as an ultimate goal the graduation of men and women dedicated to and knowledgeable about the means for bringing in a Christian social order, he will demonstrate to himself the task that opens before *Christian* education. Nor is this, immense as it is, all!

A Christian social order must be oriented to society as it is. This calls for intimate and sustained insight into the springs and ways of the world in their myriad manifestations — an insight acquired by *involvement* as well as by study. To acquire this insight, in order to "teach" it, is the task of the Christian teacher, each in his field; and having acquired it, to keep it timely and up-to-date, while transmitting it to his students as background and challenge to Christian life in the world.

The measure of achievement, the extent to which an education really has been made Christian, is ultimately the degree to which graduates seek steadfastly to form within and through the social structure of their time, the rule of God among men. But this is another subject, really.

Adam Smith and Karl Marx both supposed that amoral phenomena would, if left alone, achieve morally satisfying ends. Christianity insists that economic phenomena will achieve morally satisfying ends only if they render obedience to religious obligations.

The method of approach to economic problems varies somewhat between the two large branches of Christendom, the Protestant and the Catholic. Readers of the great Catholic encyclicals regarding the condition of labor (*Rerum novarum* of Leo XIII, and *Quadragesimo anno* of Pius XI) are more likely, if they are Protestants, to appreciate the analyses of the problem and the critique of economic liberalism than they are likely to endorse the conclusions which the Popes suggest of a kind of corporate society reminiscent of the "medieval synthesis." The same reaction is probable to Dr. Maritain's profound study of Communism and of Christian society in his *True Humanism.*

Both, however, Catholic *and* Protestant, share common ground in their determination to extend the dominion of Jesus Christ over the "laws" of economics. Both can subscribe without reservation to the admonition of Pope Pius XI, spoken by him to the Bishops of France in December, 1937: "You will convert those who are seduced by Communist doctrines in proportion as you show them that faith in Christ and love of Christ inspire devotion and goodness, in proportion as you show them that nowhere else can there be found a like source of charity. Stress this point."

Whether or not the parallel is deliberate, it is interesting to compare the Papal phraseology with that of the French Communist leader (denounced by Trotsky in his *Diary in Exile* as a "lackey" of Stalin) Maurice Thorez, who said the following at a Congress of the French Communist Party in 1938: "We shall win over to the Popular Front and to Communism those who are kept far from us by their prejudices, in so far as we show them that Communism, our noble ideal, inspires devotion and service, in so far as we show them that nowhere else will such a source of pure and generous sentiments be found."

The *choice* of master and of dynamic is clear: Christ *or* the

"noble ideal" of Communism. The task laid upon the follower
is, however, in each case strikingly similar: *"Show* them"! Telling
them is not enough! Words will not supplant deeds in persuasive
power. It is, indeed, a part of Father Chambre's interesting analysis of Communist tactics, in his book *Communism and Christianity,* to show that the Communist takes very seriously the
intimate relationship between *doing* and *believing.* William
James taught that one is afraid *because* he runs; he does not run
because he is first afraid. Whether influenced by this doctrine or
not, the Communist Party keeps its novitiates very *busy,* not only
because there is work to be done of one variety and another, but
more significantly because one comes the *more* to *believe* in a
movement the *more* he *works* for it — at least this is Communist
experience. And not Communist only.

Do and ye shall then *know* is as old as the Gospels. To persuade others by our deeds is incidentally also to deepen our own
persuasion. It is not without interest that our Lord first prescribed the *Way;* then came the *Truth;* and, at last, the *Life.*
This order of words in His description of Himself is not fortui-
tous. While it is of passing interest that the Communists ape this
insight of Christianity too, it is of imperative importance that
Christians *act* upon the deep Christian truth enunciated by the
Pope: *only* as we *show* them, shall we win them — and, so doing,
strengthen ourselves!

It is necessary to add that the Christian emphasis upon works
as evidence of faith, from which the Pope's injunction flows,
does not conflict with the primacy of the word in the procla-
mation of the Good News. It was, of course, as the word of God
that Christ enjoined His followers to *deeds* of love; and it was
by his own word that the Pope enjoined the disciples of Christ
to *show* their neighbors where their source of charity lay. Word
bears fruit in deed; deed lends authority and power to word;
and word without deed, like faith without works, is dead!

A practical illustration of a Christian approach to an economic problem presents itself, it seems to me, in that of agricultural surpluses, viewed from a national standpoint. The productivity of land is a gift of God. He has made the soil fertile. He
warms it with the sun and bathes it with the rain. Technical
skill is also a gift of God, from whom all intelligence comes. By
the combination of these two gifts, America has succeeded in
producing far more agricultural goods than it consumes, and
its potential production far exceeds what is now raised.

The answer to this economic problem by both Democratic and Republican Administrations has been to curtail agricultural production, even to pay for food not produced. Whether it is called "crop allotment" or "soil bank," the result is the same. Meanwhile it is common knowledge that hunger stalks much of the world's population, and malnutrition is not unknown in sections of our own land. Can it be that God has blessed our land with fertility, our experts with knowledge and means to increase that fertility, and given us technical skill and industrial productivity far beyond His gifts to other lands and to other peoples, simply that we may destroy our surplus or refuse to employ His bounties altogether? *If* people *are* hungry, why then is America given the gifts which together produce vast quantities of food except to *feed* the hungry?

To put it thus, simply phrases a problem. Perhaps, it may be said, this is oversimplification, and does not reckon with economic realities. School lunch programs and welfare allotments are a measure of recognition that the gift of productiveness imposes an obligation of stewardship. Shiploads of grain do go abroad, and attempts to distribute foodstuffs have been made in enough quantity to arouse protests from those nations who feared that their economies would be endangered by our largess. But the problem that hunger exists on one side of the globe while the smoke of burning produce ascends skyward (I do not say heavenward) on the other side of the globe is with us still.

It is obviously a problem to be solved only on a national scale. Whatever the means, whatever the risks, it is a good test case of whether economic "laws" rule mankind or God's commands rule economics. Let there be one hundred economic reasons — all good — why a distribution of surplus American food to the hungry of the world (say only for the moment of the *free* world, to avoid complications in the argument) *cannot* be begun tomorrow: they do not add up to *one* reason why the food received from God's hand *should not* be placed in the mouths of His creatures. Economic "law" is no apology for sin. Nor, as the failures of both Marx and of Adam Smith have demonstrated, will obedience to economic "law" bring happiness and salvation.

The task would be difficult; it would be technical. It would have political as well as economic implications. It would, like all human ventures, be stained with shortcoming. But what is necessary is the Christian statesman with the *resolution* to bring the laws of God into active dominion over the laws of economics and of politics. If the so-called Christian politician seriously intends to let the "laws" of economics dictate the way in which the morally obligatory comes to actual expression in national and international life, let him abjure the adjective "Christian" for he is but politician. If politics is the art of the possible, then *Christian statesmanship* is infusing the possible with the demands of the impossible.

Let the planning be gotten under way, guided by the best intelligence which students of political economy can provide. Let the attempt be made. And let all concerned recognize that under God the "impossible" becomes possible. Not, as I have stressed before, that we can avoid reckoning with human limitations, with social limitations, and with all the grim reality of sin in man, in society and in nature itself. But let us test the limits of the possible by the challenge of the highest and the best that we know.

No doubt the stringent application of Christian demands to the solution of economic problems has dizzying effects upon those who have supposed that Christianity is for old women, foolish boys and impractical dreamers. And, of course, the serious invasion of the "independent" sphere of economic law by Christian demands does excite surprise and perhaps indignation. No doubt it has led and will continue to lead to counterattack. For Marxism is not the only enemy of Christian "interference" in worldly affairs; the whole secular spirit for which Marxism is but one spokesman is equally adamant in its refusal to bow before Christ and His ways. But the fact remains that no gift is received but from God, and that all of His gifts to persons and to the nations which those persons constitute are intended for stewardship. If economics cannot be brought under the dominion of such stewardship, then Marx was right and economic laws *do* govern human life.

But Marx was wrong. Man is under authority in history. The question at issue between the Christian view of history and the views of economic liberalism and of Karl Marx is not one of autonomy versus servitude. It is rather one of a choice as to which god man will serve. Of the three alternatives, it is Christianity alone which because of its recognition of the image of God in man respects the right of man to choose responsibly among the options presented to him.

If he chooses economic liberalism he becomes, as Smith taught, the obedient servant of the twin masters, pleasure and pain. If he chooses Marxism, he becomes as Marx taught, the obedient servant of economic determinism. But if man recognizes that in Christianity a new dimension has broken into history, freeing him from the dominion of his desires and from the grip of necessity, he may choose freedom in obedience, and find himself in losing his all in Jesus Christ. Escaping the control of selfishness by dedicating *himself* to God, escaping the control of economic determinism by pledging *his possessions* to God in stewardship, the Christian finds that in this obedience there is freedom, peace and joy.

"Choose ye this day whom ye will serve!"

Until Christians take deeds as well as words into the market-place, their denunciations of Marx will be futile, for his strength lies in the market-place. Until we see in each man a living spirit of "more value than many sparrows," we are not really anti-Marxist. Until we see slums in terms of persons, especially of children, and not as rents or investments, we are not really anti-Marxist. Until we see world hunger in terms of God's opportunity to our charity, and God's demand for an accounting of our stewardship, we are not really anti-Marxist. Until we see factories as associations of persons, not as statistics of production, we are not really anti-Marxist. In short, until we earnestly endeavor to bring every economic relation under the dominion of love, we are not effectively engaged in anti-Marxism.

Only then may we humbly bear to those who labor in the toils of the Marxist effort to save themselves the Master's compassionate and compelling

> *Come unto me, all ye that labor*
> *And are heavy laden,*
> *And I will give you rest.*

CHAPTER 6

CHRISTIAN ANTI-COMMUNISM

IS THERE A CHRISTIAN anti-Communism, different from other anti-Communism, say secular or humanist anti-Communism? Not, surely, just for the sake of being different, but for the sake of being true to its principles, *Christian* anti-Communism may in fact be distinctive, yes! That depends, really, upon the conduct of Christian anti-Communists. Not all who say "Lord, Lord" of Jesus Christ are citizens of the Kingdom; only those who *do* His will are such citizens. No doubt not all that passes for "Christian" in the world merits God's blessing; and so Christian anti-Communisim will, finally, stand or fall unto its Lord in how it behaves.

But Christianity is different from humanism. How? In its recognition that the unique worth of man devolves upon him from God alone, while humanism thinks of man as the source of his own liberties and powers. And Christianity does differ from secularism. How? In that Christianity estimates a man as of more value than any number of things, while secularism makes man one thing among things, often the servant or slave of things, and commonly reduces human relations to what Marx aptly called the "cash nexus."

It is not so unlikely, then, that although others than Christians are anti-Communist, *Christian* anti-Communism may have a style and character quite distinct from these — not, I repeat, for the sake of being different, for this would only make it eccentric, but for the sake of being true to its own directions.

Secularism has this difficulty in confronting Communism: both place the same high estimate upon *things*. Secularism estimates the worth of man in terms of his ability to produce goods; it estimates the worth of life in terms of the accumulation of goods; and it reckons the worth of a society in terms of the kind and amount of goods it produces. Communism parallels secularism; indeed, it is the full-blown fruit of secularism, in that it estimates the worth of man first in terms of his contribution to the revolution and the new order, and, then, the worth of the new order in terms of the production and distribution it makes of goods. There is thus an inherent affinity between secularism and Communism; their measures of value are intrinsically the same. This accounts for the hysterical dread the secularist has of the Communist "menace"; he beholds in it, instinctively, a more systematic and hence more deadly organization of his own scale of values. Secularist anti-Communism has therefore a shrill and strident voice, alarmed and frantic, frightened not so much over what Communism may do to others but dreading what Communism may do to its cherished possessions. From this hysteria and self-centeredness, *Christian* anti-Communism will naturally distinguish itself, to the degree that it is true to its own foundations, and to its own spiritual rather than material scale of values.

Humanist anti-Communism, on the other hand, may speak much the same language and bear much the same mien as Christian anti-Communism, but it will seek neither its mandate nor its guidelines outside man's will and reason; and it may, in these respects, find Communist will-power and Marxist reason more than its match.

Christian anti-Communism draws its dynamic from the will of God for history, reposes its confidence in Him, and finds in His *Word* its directions. It wishes to make the alternatives clear: Christianity or Marxism.

It is noteworthy that Trotsky grew fond, in his later life, of comparing Calvinism and Communism as dynamic forces. Both, he observed, rest on the fixed assurance that the pattern of history is laid out by power superior to human will — the Calvinist finding this power in the Providence of God and the Communist finding it in dialectical materialism — and yet both Calvinist and Communist, Trotsky noted, draw from such conviction powerful impetus for human action.

It is clear that Trotsky understood the "dialectic" of Calvinism far better than some of its more superficial critics, who cannot distinguish Providence from fatalism. It is also evident that, implicitly, Trotsky himself defines the two poles between which the titanic struggles of the twentieth century oscillate: God or matter, Providence or historicism. The acknowledgment

may come hard, but is it not so: men have but two basic alternatives, the choice of the God of the Scriptures, of which John
Calvin sought to be a faithful expositor; or the choice of the
god of the "gospel according to Marx," as someone acutely put it.

Mortimer Adler has remarked that anyone who grasps the
underlying principles of Adam Smith's *Wealth of Nations* in
contrast to those principles underlying Marx's *Capital* will have
understood much of the turmoil of modern history. This is, no
doubt, correct. It is equally correct, however, to say that some
understanding of the tension in which history is moving will be
had by one who grasps the full significance of Calvin's *Institutes*
as contrasted with that of the *Communist Manifesto*.

Let us proceed without losing this perspective, to some of the
Biblical guidelines for *Christian* anti-Communism. The Christian
who does battle with Communism is pre-eminently the man of
a Book. His allegiance is to God in Christ; his guideposts are
revealed in God's written Word. There are no less than four
such Biblical guidelines.

1. SERVE THE TRUTH

This first guideline is, in fact, the spur to the very study on
which we are now engaged. We seek to know, because we are
obligated to know, the *truth* about our enemies. Simply as a
practical matter, ignorance of an enemy has never been thought
a sufficient resource for his defeat. Know your opponent as well
as, or if possible even better than, he knows himself: this is
ancient strategic advice; Demosthenes knew it well. But Christian
duty converts this advice from strategy to obligation. We must
know Communist theory and practice, not only — or even first of
all — because without such accurate knowledge we are less likely
to win our battles with Communism, but primarily because the
Christian has no right to entertain half-truths and lies, even
about his enemies! It is this stringency of obligation to the whole
truth which already distinguishes Christian anti-Communism
from some other varieties.

Knowing the whole truth about Communism obliges the Christian to acknowledge, as others may not wish to admit, that Communism has often been nurtured upon past sins of omission in
economic and social and political relations among men, sins
which the Christian Church has not always been conspicuous for
recognizing and opposing. What we are fighting, as we oppose
the march of Communism, is partly the fruit of past Christian

selfishness; what we must strive to avert is the likelihood that our children will be obliged to reap the bitter fruit of our present selfishness. Peoples the world over follow red banners in these days — the Christian must confess, in truth — at least partly because Communism promises, however cynically at times, freedoms, human dignities, economic opportunities, hopes of health, education, welfare, which the "Christian" democracies appear to be more ready to preach than to practice in international leadership.

Moreover, this honest appraisal of his context imposes upon the Christian scrupulous accuracy in his description of it. He has no right to loose talk. A Communist has, if the thesis of this book is sound, a precise and well-defined philosophy, though his tactics may change with the wind. This means that not every African native, for example, who protests colonialism, who seeks self-determination, who asks for the possession of his country's natural resources is by these tokens a Communist. And we have no right to say that he is one, unless we know that he subscribes to Marxist ideology — and unless we know what that ideology is. That those who may stand to lose power and position in Africa, Asia, South America and elsewhere if the native demands are met, that these have some stake in making the native leaders *appear* to be Communists is obvious and understandable, though not thereby justified. But the moral demand upon the Christian is unmistakable: we may not label anyone, or anything, *Communist* until first we know precisely what Communism itself implies; and, further, not until we know that this someone or something assuredly merits this classification. There are no loopholes for guesses, tactical advantages, or imposed judgments in the "Thou shalt not bear false witness . . ." under which the Christian is bound.

This is particularly true in domestic affairs. *Communist* is not today, if ever it was, an innocent adjective which can lightly be used to convey dislike, suspicion, or difference of opinion. The reckless use of *Communist* or *Communist conspiracy* or *Comsymp* or *fellow-traveler* is an affront to truth. Unless we know that such terms accurately represent the historical tendency inherent in what we denounce by them, we risk guilt of lying when we use them. Moreover, the careless use of such terminology so mystifies and confuses the real issues at stake between Communism and democracy that the real Communist — as he testifies — is helped rather than hindered in the pursuit of his objectives, while the real strength of democracy, which lies in the people's ability to choose wisely between clearly defined alternatives, is thus severely strained.

Words wear out! Rather, they are worn out. So long as words like, for example, *liberty, democracy, charity* retain relatively precise significance, they are capable of uniting men for common purposes. If, however, by indiscriminate usage they are reduced to the status of slogans, they can be employed for endlessly contradictory and confused ends; and they lose their power to unify popular action. This is happening, in reverse, to the word *Communism*. Clearly defined and understood, it musters for counter-attack all the energies of a free people. They can see the enemy and rise to meet him; the challenge, in Professor Toynbee's language, is clear; and therefore the response is forthcoming. But demeaned by reckless usage into a slogan which is used to denote not only Marxism and the Russian system, but also to condemn the income tax, racial integration, public housing, medical assistance to the aged, progressive education, decisions of the Supreme Court, actions of past Presidents of the United States, and the fluoridation of water — to name no other victims of the rash use of language — this word *Communism* loses its usefulness and its power to unite us for common action against its threat. With this traffic in confusion, whatever ends it may serve for certain limited and often selfish interests, the Christian may have nothing at all to do.

Christian anti-Communism, then, is distinguished by scrupulous accuracy of conception, great restraint in the use of its language, minute attention to fact — in short, the first Biblical guideline for *Christian* anti-Communism is: Respect the truth! Speak it! Acknowledge it! Serve it! This guideline is neither an incidental, nor, as it were, a minor injunction which, in the heat of battle or for the attaining of other "more important" ends, may be, say, temporarily ignored. It arises from the heart of Christianity itself.

Truthfulness is not, indeed, always a simple matter. Often we are hard put to know what, in a given situation, precisely is the *truth*. And this is why in the struggle we wage against Communism we can never be too much informed. But life's complexity does not diminish by one iota the gravity of a lie, *any* lie! For the lie has a devilish parentage, and a deadly patrimony. A lie is essentially an attack upon the soul of man.

Words, we must remember, are the tools by which souls are sculptured; God has made it so, and the apprehension of this truth undergirds the classical conception of a liberal education. True words make, and false words mar, the soul, both of him who speaks and of him who hears. A lie is a dreadful thing; it is the primary work of Satan. When the Bible wishes to characterize Satan, how does it do so? It speaks of him as the "father of lies" and as a "murderer from the beginning." These are related characterizations. Souls are *murdered* by lies! The *Word,* which is the *Truth,* of God saves men; the perversion of the *word,* which is a *lie,* destroys them. One does not lightly play with such issues of soul-life and soul-death. Telling the truth is enjoined from the dawn of history; it was, indeed, a lie neatly disguised as truth which perverted human history at its source.

The power of Christianity springs up out of the Truth, and is made into a creative historical force to the extent that human lips and lives echo truth. We will not outwit Satan, in whatever historical form we encounter him, with weapons he has used longer than we. If this ultimate and radical importance of truth-telling is ignored, the struggle against Communism as a religion is vitiated at the outset. Anti-Communism, if it is *Christian,* may not attempt to weaken, for the attainment of apparently valid or easy ends, or for any other reason, the absolute stringency of *Thou shalt not bear false witness. . . !* No, not even in regard to real Communists themselves! to say nothing of fellow Americans, fellow Christians, or the struggling masses of the world who mistakenly turn to Communism as their angel of hope and light!

2. EXAMINE SELF

Christian anti-Communism is distinguished, secondly, by the attitude it takes toward itself, and toward the struggle in which it is engaged. It asks: *why? Why* is this massive threat thrust so clearly upon us all? *Why* is the threat of Communism writ so large that none cannot see?

John Calvin, who had some firsthand experience with threats, and who frequently counseled others whose lives were endangered, answered such questions in this way: "As soon as we feel any chastisement, of whatsoever kind it may be, the first step should be to retire into ourselves, and well to examine our own lives. . . . To consider and look into ourselves, that we may acknowledge that we have well deserved on our part to receive such visitation, to chastise our negligence, our contempt, and our careless slighting of the word of God among us."

He says, notice, "first of all." This *first of all* is not coincidental. Without *it* the "second" and the "third" steps, whatever they may be in the struggle, are less than likely to succeed. It is God who threatens His children — whether by Nebuchadnezzar or by Khrushchev — with imminent peril, *for their own good!* The threat is designed. It is meant to be *instructive.* Its goal is self-examination, not as an end in itself but as the first step to self-correction.

Observe that Calvin does not propose that we turn "first of all" to a scrutiny of someone else. We are not "first of all" to bemoan the worldliness of our neighbors. They, if they understand the meaning of the Communist threat — and this *meaning* we surely must explain to them — are obligated, then, like us, "first of all" to *self*-examination. After the beam is out of our own eye, only then our Lord told us, are we to deal with the moat in someone else's.

Now, Communism's threat is a *total* threat; it is aimed at our whole way of life — economic, social, political, religious. This must mean that God calls upon us to examine our total way of life, both personal and national — in all its economic, social, political, and religious facets. Not of course for the sake of the examination only, but for setting to work at correcting those sins God has detected, for this is why He threatens us. And this self-examination and self-correction are indispensable to winning the world-wide struggle against Communism; because the image which America presents to the world, an image which will — we hope — attract peoples to our side, depends for its lustre and magnetic power upon our developing success in making democracy operative and Christianity relevant here at home.

To do this we need not minimize our notable achievements as a free people; to do that would be to ignore God's great blessings upon us. Ours is now, by grace, the last best hope of mankind in action; we need not, may not, sell it short. Nowhere are so many so free. Nowhere is progress in human welfare taken more seriously.

But if, nonetheless, God finds it necessary to threaten our way of life with the total destruction of atomic war, then we obviously have sins to confess, crimes to expiate, tasks to get at; beginning with none more urgent than our national forgetting that all of our blessings come from the hand of God, and are to be used in

His service and the love of our neighbors; and not only of our neighbors within our borders, in this one world we have made! If we have as a nation prospered beyond man's dreams, we have unfortunately been laggard in sharing this immense wealth with the great masses of the world's poverty-stricken. Do we not kennel our dogs and stable our horses in greater comfort than many parents are able to provide for the shelter of their children? Do we not take from the world in raw materials more readily than we return to it finished goods? How is it that we dare restrict our production of food while *God's children* around the world cry daily for bread? Do we suppose that this weeping ascends in vain to heaven?

And rich as we are at home, free as we are, powerful as we are, this threat warns us that, although measured by other nations we have come far, measured by the demands of the Kingdom of God among men we have yet far to go. All this, and more, the "first of all" of *Christian* anti-Communism will demand of us.

The failure to heed this demand, the refusal to recognize the Communist threat as first of all admonitory, is dangerous if not fatal. The Chosen People missed the import of God's warnings by threats from powerful neighbors, even with the prophets there to interpret these threats in vivid and powerful language; and they went from captivity to final dispersion. Shall we not say that Western man must have missed the import of God's warning by means of World War I, that the godlessness, inequities, barbarities, miseries, and gross sins concealed by the facade of civilization demanded repentance, atonement, correction? And in time much of that facade was itself burned out by fire bombs rained down from the sky in World War II.

Will we as individuals and as a nation now first of all examine our ways, take to our knees, sell and give, strive for practical correction of our sins — or must a more terrible and destructive fire cleanse the earth we cannot keep clean by ourselves? This is the question Communism poses as unwitting agent of the God of history. Do we, any more than the Communists themselves whose blindness we deplore, see the signs, descrie the meaning, and tremble?

No anti-Communism can be genuinely *Christian* in its inspiration, intent, or consequences if it misses the element of judgment in the present crisis. Of course, a secular or humanist anti-Communism will fight desperately for its way of life; but this fight becomes *Christian* in its inspiration when this way of life is itself brought to judgment, first of all, in the world-wide struggle against the Marxist foe.

Organized Christianity, too, is threatened by Communist atheism. To the Church, too, comes God's injunction to self-examination. What will the Christian Church say as it contemplates the shameful truth that there have been, in the last century, men motivated by the highest human ideals for social and economic justice, men moved by a most profound compassion for the poor and the oppressed, men capable of astounding abnegation and self-denial, that *such* men (not brigands, villians, or scoundrels), seeking desperately for a channel through which to pour their energies and their aspirations rejected organized Christianity and were driven to the illusions of Communism? The Christian anti-Communist who ignores this historical judgment, or who evades its condemnation by reference — true enough in itself — to the mysterious force of the demonic in history, such a Christian has not fully grasped the meaning of the fact that Communism arose as a *substitute* faith, as a competing religion which took on much of its magnetism by professing to deal with practical moral problems in human relations which organized Christianity too often preferred then, and prefers now, to ignore. It is as a religion that Communism has been able to attract, though usually not to hold, many of its idealistic adherents, who are later disillusioned by the bitter experience of the emptiness of its pretenses.

But let us not forget that the threat which Communism poses to Christianity now is God's reminder that the disillusioned Communist turned to his false god in the first place because the true God was not as effectually represented in the world as He might have been. Nor let us turn away from the meaning to be read out of the truth, that even today men most deeply concerned with social justice are obliged to find channels for their enthusiasm in wholly secular institutions, platforms for views in wholly secular forums, support for their enterprises largely in secular movements. Communist threats to the Church are God's reminder that its words will be tried by its deeds; and that its deeds must bear out its claims to represent God among the consciences of men, if the Church is to engross the faith and energies of noble minds and sensitive hearts in this generation.

Christians may not hear from their pulpits as frequently as they might the penetrating social and economic implications of the gospel; but these omissions do not alter the will of God for history, they do not change the social implications of salvation. They simply point up the dereliction of the Church to the social dimensions of its message.

Too frequently the Church as moral monitor has allowed itself to be bluffed out of the market-place, leaving the ebb and sway of the market-place to the "laws" of economics. This failure has even been called *Christian* economics, the free play of supply and demand being conceived as the "secret harmony" sustained by the very God whose Body in history, the living Church, is barred from judging either the players or the game itself. "A whole pseudo-scientific school of conservative anarchists in economics directly denied, and still denies, though without the old self-confidence, all ethical principles and all organization in the sphere of economic relations," wrote the Russian Christian philosopher, Solovyof, in 1896; and he added, significantly: "The prevalence of this school had much to do with the birth of revolutionary anarchism." Not only "had" but, we may now add, "would have" much more to do, in Solovyof's Russia, with revolutionary anarchism.

Solovyof continues, as acutely: "On the other hand, the many varieties of socialism, both radical and conservative, do more to detect the presence of the disease than to offer a real cure for it." How true! The "real cure" does not lie in socialism, nor in any other of man's constructions. It lies in the power of the gospel, when that power is consciously applied to economic relationships. This is no secret. Christian men and women in countless business relationships control the "laws" of economics by the power of their faith. But we will have no Christian *society*, no approximation of the full power of the kingdom of God among men until these sporadic individual efforts receive unification, continuing inspiration, and dedicated leadership from organized Christianity, if not officially as the Church, then under the immediate guidance of the Church.

Too often this leadership has been left to a theological liberalism which derives its dynamic as much from humanism as from the gospel, while the orthodox whose feet are planted on firmer Ground have betrayed that inability to cope with vast secular problems which so typifies fundamentalism. In short, where the enthusiasm for social justice is, the power of the full gospel is diluted; and where the power of the gospel stands ready, the will to involve it in the daily, dirty, complex issues of economic life is weak or frustrated.

It is of such things as these that the judgment imposed by the Communist alerts the Christian Church. And if we heed not, the prophetic words of Solovyof may ring in our ears: "Free play of chemical processes can only take place in a corpse; in a living body these processes are connected and determined by organic purposes. Similarly, free play of economic factors and laws is only possible in a community that is dead and is decomposing, while in a living community that has a future, economic elements are correlated with and determined by moral ends. To proclaim *laissez faire, laissez passer,* is to say to society 'die and decompose.' "

Solovyof's society chose to be decomposed. In America, let us give thanks, we are choosing otherwise. But is the social legislation which has stayed the blind hand of economic "law" been as much the product of *Christian* concern, Christian invasion of this forbidden terrain, as it has been in response to essentially humanist demands, only indirectly empowered by the gospel?

In brief, Communism calls us all to self-examination, "first of all," if we are effectively to contest it as a pseudo-religion. Guideline number two for *Christian* anti-Communism is: self-examination, judgment, correction: personal, national, religious.

3. DISCERN THE REAL ENEMY

We speak of Communism and Communists as *The Enemy.* Popular anti-Communism bids us rise and destroy *The Enemy.* This kind of talk sets many of us to thinking of how easy it might be just to drop a bomb here and there . . . just as, long ago, James and John, "Sons of Thunder," proposed to call down fire from heaven upon a Samaritan village which shut its doors upon our Lord. But it was a solution the Master rebuked. "Ye know not what spirit ye are of," He said. Do we know what spirit we are of in our anti-Communism?

Again, *Christian* anti-Communism turns to a Biblical guideline, one I shall define as: discern the *real* enemy as you struggle against the Communist! This discernment reveals that the historical, visible contest between Communism and Christianity is but one conspicuous facet of the fundamental spiritual contest between God and Satan for possession of the bodies and souls of men. This contest was touched off in Paradise, and motivates history itself. God wants His children; Satan seeks to constrain unto himself their allegiance. The embodiment of this radical competition is history.

It would be easier to discuss this bitter contest were one permitted to define it as fought only over the *souls,* and not the bodies, of men. Just as it would be easier to obey the commandment to love our neighbors if it were only their souls we were supposed to love. One might go into raptures over his passion for the welfare of his neighbor's soul if the measure of his sincerity were not to be gauged by his compassion for the neighbor's body. The failure to recognize that God has made man both body and soul, and that both are to be redeemed, was the fatal defect of the Holy Inquisition, which for the sake of men's souls practiced innumerable barbarities upon men's bodies, to the brutalization of victim and Inquisitor both. Man is body and soul. History reflects the struggle between God and Satan for both body and soul; this is why flight from history, by a monasticism of body or of intellect, is at enmity with the purpose of God in time.

God authenticated the significance of the daily, visible, palpable, interrelationships of tangible bodies by the Incarnation. Christ came not as idea — to believe this is the temptation of all rationalisms — but as man, with a body like unto our own, a body since risen to heaven in full view of His disciples' wondering eyes. Thus did daily, bodily life receive its true significance, and ideas get set in their proper, ancillary place as servants of life.

The eruption, then, of the battle now being waged between Communism and Christianity must be understood in terms of the real combatants: Satan and God; and in terms of the servants of these powers: the sons of men.

The Christian is aware at once, when his anti-Communism is set in this perspective, that his own life is itself a battleground and he is never free from sins of his own doing. This awareness, this inability to view himself as wholly "sheep" and those he confronts in history as wholly "goat," chastens the Christian's invective and tempers his judgment. He is himself saved only by grace, and his own best deeds — yea, even his own anti-Communism — are marred by imperfection.

His real strength deriving from God, the Christian views his real enemy as God's archfoe, Satan. The final objective of *Christian* anti-Communism is therefore the defeat of Satan, even in the hearts of the Communists themselves. To return evil for evil is to multiply the work of Satan, even if done under the banners of the Lord. Christian anti-Communism cannot stop short of bringing the Communist into the camp of God. This is the victory over Communism at which we aim.

But our battle with Communism is waged in history. Communism is not only a theory; it is embodied in Communists. The contest is not only between ideas but is a contest between spiritual powers incarnate in men. This is the complication upon which we have already reflected.

Against our will, it happens that men seek to settle their contests by war. War is, for the Christian, the ultimate inability to distinguish between men of flesh and blood, with whom St. Paul tells us we do not wrestle, and the demons whose instruments men become. War is thus the unmistakable objectification of the human predicament. In war we cannot maintain the distinction between the spiritual enemy whom we would destroy in the name of the Lord, and the human "enemy" whom we would save in the name of the Lord. In war we have no option left: kill or be killed.

This predicament roots in the fact, which we have stressed, that God defined *history* as the material embodiment of spirit; and man perverted history by admitting into its course the influence of a spirit alien to God. Since that Fall man has been caught in the web of his own history, a web tangling and entangled by the presence of Satan in man's heart and deeds. Our rescue from the historical contradictions which war so hideously illustrates can only come, and has only come, by God's invasion of the web — by God's allowing himself to become entangled in the web — through the Incarnation. But this rescue is itself not fully consummated until the web has exacted from us, too, our mortal lives; and so long as our pilgrimage is in history, so long will our sins, though forgiven, be many. We cannot do perfectly, as we ought.

Indeed, man's most massive efforts to free himself from the web that binds him, made in the great revolutions which have convulsed history, have only in the end multiplied his entanglements. The French Revolution announced *liberty, equality, fraternity,* to a nation which knew little enough of these. Moreover, the revolutionaries meant what they promised, at least at first. Their promises stirred the souls of the poor, the maimed, the halt, and the blind. They loosed mighty energies which uprooted the old regime. And then, all too soon, the Revolution turned to devouring its own leadership and closed by delivering the nation into the hands of Napoleon. So, again, the Russian and Chinese Revolutions, titanic eruptions of hopes smoldering deep in hearts grown almost alien to hope, became almost at once the tomb of these and the chains reforged upon them. In his *Literature and Revolution,* Leon Trotsky dilates brilliantly upon the "new man" which the Communist Revolution will usher into history. Do we need more evidence than Trotsky's own tragic end and the brutal course his revolution has run to teach us that humanism, even of the superlative quality of Trotsky's, is not enough to cut the bands by which man is bound?

Though we cannot free ourselves of the toils of history, it is (by God's grace) true that we have, short of war, options we can exercise in Christian anti-Communism.

We can strive to persuade mankind to reject the Communist political system, and to prefer some form of democracy in its stead; not as an end in itself, but as providing the best climate for the spread of the rule of God among men.

We can strive to persuade men to reject the Communist economic and social structure, and to develop a free and un-regimented society; not, again, as an end in itself, but as affording the best opportunities for the extension of a Christian social order.

And, because history is so ordained — once more — that deeds bear out words, and faith without works is no faith, we will be most *persuasive* when we are most *active* in demonstrating that Christianity does lead to God's rule among ourselves. This is not to say that words are in themselves vain; St. James does not say that faith is *in itself* fruitless; on the contrary, without words and without faith, there would be no confirming deeds. God has simply so construed history, that words and beliefs demonstrate their *own power and validity* in their consequences. The test is history! The Word became flesh, and our Master went about doing good. In His flesh He bore our stripes for our healing. If God took so seriously the relation of body to spirit, the *meaning* of history, the translation of Word into Deed — dare we do less?

Moreover, we will oppose with all our energies the outbreak of war, because in war we are limited so severely in our responses to our enemies. Not that we are obliged to choose the way of pacifism, though I do not wish to enter upon any extended discussion of that involved subject. "All are to blame for everything," Dostoyevsky said, and pacifism must be directed at this

CHRISTIAN ANTI-COMMUNISM   133

grim fact, if it is not to be a flight from its own complicity in society's crimes. War comes because all of us have, bit by bit, made it sometimes possible, sometimes inevitable. After it has come, no pacifistic flight from its awful holocaust can absolve us of responsibility for participation in its origins. It might be argued, and that upon Biblical evidence, that we are to expiate our responsibility by refusing to meet force with force, and thus to await, like the Elders of Jerusalem before their Roman conquerers, with folded arms our execution. To this suggestion we will return.

Let us sum it all up by reminding ourselves that in history we wrestle with flesh and blood only as the embodiment of spiritual forces locked in deadly contest for eternal possession of men. Unless we set our anti-Communism in this dimension, it is hardly *Christian* anti-Communism. The third guideline then is: discern the Devil as the *real enemy* in every battle against sin.

4. LOVE YOUR ENEMIES

In the perspective established now, the injunction to love our enemies and to do good to those who persecute us becomes more easily intelligible. Calvin wrote to the Church of Strasbourg, and to the Duchess of Ferrara, "Wherefore my brethren, if you seek true victory, do not oppose evil by evil of a like kind . . . for we ought chiefly to desire that all those who are now at enmity with Christ may be brought to a willing obedience to Him, rather than conquered by force of arms, but not corrected. For the remedy is to hate evil without taking persons into account, striving to do good to those who are unworthy of it, just as God causes his sun to shine on the evil and the good. Thus hatred and Christianity are things incompatible. I mean hatred towards persons. . . . On the contrary, we are to wish and even procure their good, and to labor, as much as in us lies, to maintain peace and concord with all men."

Christian anti-Communism must be waged in *love!* Love must enable us to be always and fully aware that the Communist is a person, destined for eternity in body and soul, called even at this hour by God to repentance. Of this we are obliged to remind him by word and by deed; in the Church of our Lord Jesus Christ the Communist must see indubitably the arms of the Lord's Body stretched forth still, beckoning, welcoming, pleading, inviting! These arms must be our own!

Had we ever supposed that *Christian* anti-Communism finds expression in the casting of a stone, in passing by on another side, in dropping an atomic bomb? To call the Lie a *lie*: this is indeed our duty; but never in isolation from the call to repentance in the words of love! A Christian, I have maintained, need not try to be "different" for the sake of being conspicuous; but if *his* anti-Communism is not conspicuous by being more than threat, more than denunciation, more than criticism — I do not say it must be less — he must consider if *his* anti-Communism is *Christian* at all.

Baffling? Yes, our Lord knows! Impossible? It may be.

But we are required, without qualification, to love our enemies. This is not necessarily to "like" them, or their ways; but *love* is, surely, not less than a settled design for their eternal good, a good which the Incarnation reminds us is inseparable from their *temporal* affairs.

"If thine enemy hunger. . . ." Then what? Rejoice? Tell him that his way of life is thus proclaimed inadequate? Yes, no doubt tell him that — though without rejoicing. Starvation is also a judgment from God. It may well teach its victims that their way of life needs correction; a judgment in which, no doubt, they will readily concur; their question will be, what does famine teach our rulers? But for us this interplay between the starving and God does not alter the Biblical instruction: "Feed him"! No blinding our eyes to starvation, least of all starvation among our *enemies*. This is what the Bible says.

Do armies run on their stomachs, and food therefore empowers the enemy? I do not deny it. But army generals may be forgiven for viewing enemies in a glass darkly — they derive their duties from that ultimate impasse of human contradiction, war! We, who are not army generals, have less excuse to plead for our sins; if thine *enemy* hunger . . . !

Will we try to explain away the force of this command, now, in international relations? And still call *our* anti-Communism *Christian?* Or will we obey as best we can, and acknowledge that God drives us thus to our knees! and to further good works! As Americans, unalterably persuaded of the virtues of democracy, we will protect it by keeping — and if necessary by using — our atomic weapons. But behold, there on the atomic stockpile! Is that not Christian fallen to his knees? And is he not praying for himself and his sins — and for his enemies!

At the least, this consciousness of our duty to love, and of our inability fully to do so, will give to our anti-Communism a tone unmistakable in its sobriety and discipline. Our concern for the person of the enemy, however inadequate to the high demands of divine law, will show through. No denunciation without also invitation! No judgment of others more incisive and penetrating than our judgment of ourselves! No word or deed unconstrained by an ever-present awareness of the obligations of charity.

Nor will we permit the dimensions of world-wide struggle to dilute our sense of personal responsibility. To quote Solovyof once more: "If the elementary moral feeling of pity, which has received its highest sanction in the Gospel, demands that we should feed the hungry, give drink to the thirsty, and warm the cold, this demand does not, of course, lose its force when the cold and hungry number millions instead of dozens. And if *alone* I cannot help these millions, and am not therefore morally bound to do so, I can and must help them *together with others*. My personal duty becomes a collective one — it still remains my own, although it becomes wider in so far as I participate in the collective whole and its universal task." Our duty to love takes on institutional dimensions when our personal world is set, as it is more and more, in the one world our technological progress has made. This staggering extension of demands upon our love must drive us to organizing our works of love on an equal scale.

Finally, I return briefly to the discussion broached above about pacifism. I suggested there that pacifism as an attempt to disengage ourselves from responsibility for the horrors of war comes a little late, for wars are brought about, by deeds done and undone, long before they are declared, through the complicity of us all. Mankind is corporately involved in sin, for mankind comes as an organic unity from the hand of God. Individuals are saved because the Atonement is sufficient for *man;* and the Atonement had to be sufficient for *man* because *all* men are involved in *man's* sins. "No man," Donne wrote, "is an island." Therefore, pacifism as an escape is an illusion.

But there is another ground for pacifism. It resides in the fact that our salvation was purchased by vicarious suffering. An innocent Victim died for the sins of others. Are we not to try to follow Him also in this, that we suffer for sins we are not conscious of having committed? This, too, is *love,* greater love than any other, to take upon oneself the chastisement of another's sins.

How, from this point of view, we are to conduct ourselves *vis à vis* the Communist whose sins we denounce is a fundamental Christian problem each must face for himself. Ghandi rejected the gospel because not enough of its adherents took the way of self-denial, even to the point of non-resistance to evil. For many of us this way demands too much. But the pattern set by our Lord is hardly mistakable: by way of suffering He brought in the Kingdom. However we seek to apply this truth to our lives, our anti-Communism cannot be closed to this dimension: Communism arose and flourishes upon our sins, whatever may be other sources of its power. To expect that we can oblige the Communist alone to bear the suffering for those sins is a practical denial of fundamental lessons taught by the words and deeds of our Master. A Christian pacifism informed by this conception of Christian duty is heroic, and palatable but to the few. For us all, however, the fourth guideline is clear: love your enemies!

A Positive Program

The whole world has a stake in the success of anti-Communism. This is so because the extension of the dominion of the red flag over peoples, tribes, and nations has been the extension of the dominion of slavery, often of body and always of mind and soul. However enlightened may be the ideals of individual Communists, the attempted translation of these ideals into reality has always been made by constant reference to a lexicon of censorship, exile, firing squads, forced labor, gallows, and prisons. The race has been to the swift, the brutal, the ruthless. It is the world, therefore, which has much to gain from Communism's loss.

But negation, defeat, is not enough. To sweep the soul clean of demons, but to replace these with nothing better, invites, as our Lord told us, only more demons to return. Were every Communist converted to anti-Communism tomorrow, what then? Do not pass the question lightly by! To answer it will oblige us to ask if we are not only *against* Communism, but if we are *for* anything else. It is said that a South American peasant explained his turning to Communism by saying that the only men he knew who seemed interested in helping him get a decent roof over his children's heads were Communists. Who will be interested in decent roofs for peasant families, around the world, when the Communists are gone? What are we *for?* in South America? in Africa? in Asia?

Defining ourselves only in terms of what we are *against,* if indulged in long enough, atrophies our ability to define what we want to be for. Books are easy to come by written by authors who find themselves unable to take any position unless it is over against someone else. This becomes a mental disease. It might become a national disease. America has grown used to formulating its national purposes in the language of opposition: in the thirties we were against the Depression; in the forties we were against Fascism; in the fifties we were against Communism. We needed to be against these things, no doubt of that; but what purposes have we which are not oriented to what we are *against?*

It should be, really, the other way around, and we may as a nation be thankful that it in a measure is: what we are against ought to be defined reflexively by what we are for. For this reason the guidelines I have enumerated are positive guidelines, drawn between the twin stars of Truth and Love. We cannot set a course for life, either as persons or as a nation, by the black stars of falsehood or of hatred, nor of pride nor of evil.

If we are Christian, we are anti-Communist; not just to be anti-Communist, but because Christianity is doctrinally at the antipodes from Marxism. God and atheism do not mix. Even when we concede that Communism calls the world's attention to problems of suffering, exploitation, and injustice which might otherwise be too lightly ignored, Christianity is diametrically opposed to Communism.

But this opposition does not define Christianity; it is a by-product. The most constructive social force in human history is, and has been, the Christian religion, not only as a thing active in its own right but also as the real dynamic in liberating movements which officially denied the connection. And it will be as the Christian Church reassumes its dominant role in the world that Communism will be, as by the way, pushed aside. The Church's whispers must become shouts, its lethargy must become enthusiasm, its subdued light must become a beacon set upon the hilltops of the world! Then will Communism be rolled back, by an anti-Communism which is, as it were, the rolling wake of a vessel bound in another direction.

And unless some such positive program informs our conduct

and extends our horizon, anti-Communism itself can become a frustrating thing. Consider the citizen who attends an anti-Communist rally. He becomes emotionally aroused to a sense of "something rotten in the state of Denmark." But he has received no precise notion of what that "something" is, nor of who might be responsible for it, nor of what might be done about it. He goes home filled with grim determination to be up and doing, without knowing what to do except to arouse other citizens to similar purposeless pugnacity. He soon gets the galling feeling of beating fruitlessly about in the air, and may take to populating the air with "conspiracy" to escape being more than a little silly. He is tempted to personalize his suspicions in his Congressman, his minister, the schools, unknown manipulators, or even his wife. He takes to looking under his bed for menacing red men, and exudes the air of impending calamity.

All of this because he really has nothing to do. What can he do, this aroused American, to drive out Communism? It is not likely, the F.B.I. being the efficient organization that it is, that the "Commies" are lying in wait to take over America on some scheduled doomsday, though the speaker at the rally hints that he knows the secret time-table. But even if they were, our bewitched citizen will not find them skulking around City Hall, the radio stations, and the water works. What *can* he do?

This citizen victim of mass hypnosis may even come to suspect that strategic posts in our national government are occupied, or influenced by, master spies from behind the Iron Curtain. He comes to blaming them for every national misfortune, and cannot understand why the President is not gifted with his superior insight into the deceptions practiced under his very nose. Everything becomes a part of the "Communist conspiracy," from bad turns in the weather to bad turns on the stock market.

What is wrong with this not altogether hypothetical American citizen is that he has received an overdose of "Anti-ism," and is underfed on what America is *for*. He, like poor Rip Van Winkle, has quaffed too frequently at the cup, the cup of negativism; and, like Rip, he may well be asleep for twenty years to the positive demands of citizenship.

The best anti-Communism will come not only out of a determined opposition to all that Communism stands for, but it will come, even more so, out of the best dedication to the goals of freedom, of justice, of equity, of brotherhood, of the Christian life. To dedicate himself to these goals, the citizen need not look for Communists in his linen closets, nor at the right hand of public servants, nor in the nation's capital. Rather, let him practice truth and righteousness in his daily life; let him attend with diligence to the duties of citizenship; let him alert himself to the currents moving in the world; let him learn wherein Communism deludes, and the answer to its pretenses; let him work, write, talk, live for the realization of freedom, justice, brotherhood in his community, in his state and nation, and for the world.

The doing of these things is the undoing of Communism. The spread of the gospel of our Lord is the dispersion of the "gospel" of Marx. The spread of freedom is the shrinkage of tyranny. The flow of love is the ebb of hate. The triumph of God is the defeat of Satan.

CHAPTER 7

ANTI-COMMUNISM BOOK LIST

WHAT SHALL I READ about Communism? This question occurs with increasing frequency; and so it should. Time was, not so long ago, when the study of Marxism required defence. The prevailing mood was then one of suspicion. Too many Americans seemed ready to suppose that those who made some acquaintance with Marxist dogma would at once prefer it to American principles. Happily this lack of faith in democracy predominates no longer. Authoritative voices like that of J. Edgar Hoover have warned "each citizen" that he has a "duty to learn more about the menace that threatens his future, his home, his children, the peace of the world. . . ." Anti-Communist "schools" draw ever larger crowds, and discussion groups on Communism arise on campuses and in communities.

Except for the vain hope that Communism can be mastered in ten lectures, half a dozen pamphlets, or the viewing of one or two films, all of this interest in *learning* about our enemy evidences a healthy reaction to growing tensions. We have accepted the fact that Communism cannot be conjured out of the world by denunciation alone, and we recognize that it cannot be defeated by ignorance of its philosophy and teaching.

Communism is not, in reality, preferable in any sense to democratic capitalism; Communism is in practice a hideously brutal form of dictatorship; Communism is the cruel ape of religion in arousing hopes and feeding upon aspirations it can only frustrate and destroy. These things being so, the victory over Communism inherent in a vital Christianity can be realized on innumerable fronts where Christian and Communist meet, largely to the extent that Christians *know* their enemy and *practice* what they preach.

This knowing one's enemy is an arduous business. The litera-

140

ture which has sprung from the soil first tilled by Marx little more than a century ago is now enormous. No one can read it all, least of all each citizen whose duty it is to grasp something of the intent of his foe. The selection of books which follows is intended to help those who take their duty seriously enough to surrender a little recreation, or who will devote less time to *The Saturday Evening Post* or *Ladies' Home Journal* for a year or two in exchange for study. I rather think our enemies and many "neutrals" all over the world do just this. Will you?

But what, then, to read? and where to begin? There are, no doubt, countless satisfactory answers to these questions. I can offer only my own. If it is in any way useful to you, let us join the growing number of Americans, indeed of persons all over the world, dedicated in the name of one Lord and one passion for liberty to the confrontation and defeat of a malignancy which threatens us and our children.

The books listed below are, I believe, in print, that is, available through a bookseller; very many of them are now published in inexpensive paperbound editions; all or most of them are probably in some library available to you. There is one point to remember: this is, in a way, a *reading-course*. It has a beginning and an end. It moves from *understanding* Marxism on through the *Christian refutation* of it. You need not, of course, stay on the train through its whole journey, nor need you pause in each of the cars as recommended; but if you get off half-way there is the risk that you will not get to your intended destination at all, and you may have a confused view of the landscape you have traversed in its relation to the kind of world you hoped to see.

INTRODUCTION

1. Isaiah Berlin. *Karl Marx.* New York, Oxford University Press, 1939.

This is the best single volume on the life and teaching of Karl Marx that I know. It was written for the Home University Library, an indication that it is directed to "everyman" for his spare time. Karl Marx, you must remember, lived on *hope,* and for that hope endured awful poverty. His hope was to guide the world out of poverty and all its concomitants. That in fact his guidance led to the most brutal and systematic of all dictatorships was not his intention, though it was, I think, his fault for supposing that men can redeem themselves. But you will not understand him if you confuse his *hope* with the dictatorship's crunching destruction of hope; remember rather that his hope was the torch to which millions turned, not aware that its brilliance would become "darkness at noon." That is, you will understand Marx best if you remember that he aimed at "heaven"; he did not guess, as we know, that he would set history in motion in another direction.

THE ECONOMIC BACKGROUND

2. Robert L. Heilbroner. *The Worldly Philosophers*. New York, Simon & Schuster, 1953.

Marx asserted that his system arose from the facts of economics and is validated by them. So, getting a little background in economics has its uses for us, and it is interestingly provided by this volume, which includes a useful chapter on Marx. A more careful study of the classical economists Malthus, Ricardo, and Adam Smith can follow from Heilbroner's "Guide to Further Reading," if you care to pursue it. Marx leaned on all three of these theorists to such an extent that he has been charged with contributing nothing new to their teaching. He simply compounded classical economic theory into a ferment of his own brewing. This is very likely true; and, incidentally, accounts for the fact that the real criticism of Marxism is rarely confined to his economic theory. Were his theory refuted in all its facets, much of the foundation upon which capitalist practice stands would also be called to question. So one needs a broader scope for both the understanding and the criticism of Marxism than is afforded by economics, and this leads to the next division.

THE PHILOSOPHICAL BACKGROUND

Trotsky has said that without Hegel, that vast and forbidding German thinker, Marx could not have existed. This tantalizing bit sends one scurrying to the shelves for Hegel, who soon enough sends him scurrying back for air. Unless your wish to understand Marx in all his facets has deep roots, the early chapters in Berlin's *Karl Marx,* which you might now wish to re-read, will unite clearly enough the Hegelian and the economic trends in Marxism. If you want to go further, the Edmund Wilson title which follows pursues the ideological background to Marxism from the point of view of "history," which as a philosophical study also owes much to Hegelianism. Some have found

Wilson "brilliant"; I find him sometimes also tedious. Suit yourself. If you will "have at" Hegel himself, try numbers 4 to 6.

3. Edmund Wilson. *To the Finland Station*. New York, Doubleday, 1953 (Anchor book).

4. W. T. Stace. *The Philosophy of Hegel*. New York, Dover Publications.

5. Hegel's "Introduction" to his Lectures on the History of Philosophy. New York, Dover Publications.

6. Hegel's "Introduction" to his Lectures on the Philosophy of History. New York, The Liberal Arts Press.

If you find yourself bogged down in Hegel, be not dismayed; you keep excellent and numerous company. Promise yourself that you will return one day, and go on. At least you know the name now, and can join a good deal of other "scholarship" in running a good bluff a long way. Let's try the master himself.

KARL MARX

Reading *about* Marx is no substitute for reading Marx himself. This is true of all significant books, and this is why the claptrap of manuals, guides, and textbooks which do not lead you to the sourcebooks, the "great" books, are pernicious and stultifying.

But Marx is dull! So one reads. He is a vast desert relieved by only an occasional oasis! If you believe this, you have in store the delight of finding lucid exposition, passionate and powerful prose, moving documentation of human ills, well and carefully selected in number 7. Marx did not play at convictions, nor did he talk one way and live another. It is inevitable, then, that such a man should write from the depths of the soul he denied having. He can be technical, abstruse, bitter, scornful; but leave the legend that he is dull to those who don't read him. This one volume is enough to get the "flavor" and to grasp the leading themes:

7. Karl Marx. *Capital and Other Writings*. New York, Random House, 1932 (Modern Library).

THE MARXISTS

If a genius exacts from those who follow him the task of understandng him, it is the fate of most followers not to agree in this "understanding." Hegel's ardent disciples split into two streams: a "Left," which found in Hegelianism the motive force for revolution, and a "Right," which found in the same Hegelianism a bulwark of autocracy and the status quo. The "Marxists" also split into two streams: a "Left," which headed for violent revolution, guided by Kautsky, Plekhanov, Trotsky, and Lenin; and a "Right," which sought constitutional and social reforms, guided by Bernstein and Jaures. All quoted Marx as their scriptures; all donned his mantle and clutched it tightly about themselves. To them all, even before he died, the grim old man shouted, "I am no Marxist!" Had he lived to the era of Stalin, he would have not so much shouted as wept.

The best summary of the "Marxists," which includes selections from their own writings, is number 8.

Some selection from their numerous publications is inevitable unless you have a good deal of time at your disposal, and even more patience. Lenin's works rank highest in influence, and he is probably more quoted now in Communist literature than is Marx. His most important works are these: *Materialism and Empirico-Criticism* (1909), a philosophical treatise; *Imperialism* (1917), a development of Marx's belief that capitalism led inexorably to the exploitation of colonial nations and thence to world war; and *State and Revolution,* a blueprint for revolt written while Lenin was engineering one, and published in 1918. Each to his taste, but I prefer for a sample of Lenin an earlier booklet, listed as number 9. It is not only a sustained attack on Bernstein's "deviation," but a program for action written back in the days (1902) when the assurance of success seemed far away.

Stalin wrote heavily, if he wrote his own material at all. A taste of him is enough — more than enough if you are in a hurry — except, and this is an important "except," his ponderous grayness of style reflects truly enough the grim leveling-off which planning salvation by dictatorship is bound to imply. Kautsky, interestingly, concerned himself with religious "communism." I add the title as another facet of the "mind" of Marxism.

8. Sidney Hook. *Marx and the Marxists.* New York, Van Nostrand, 1955.

9. V. I. Lenin. *What is to be Done?* New York, International, 1920.

10. J. Stalin. *Foundations of Leninism.* New York, International, 1930.

11. K. Kautsky. *Communism in Central Europe in the Time of the Reformation.* New York, Russell, 1959.

THE RUSSIAN REVOLUTION

12. Bertram Wolfe. *Three Who Made a Revolution*. Boston, Beacon, 1955.

13. Leon Trotsky, *The History of the Russian Revolution*. New York, Simon & Schuster, 1932-34.

14. John Reed. *Ten Days that Shook the World*. New York, Random House, 1935.

15. Hugh Seton-Watson. *From Lenin to Khrushchev*. New York, Praeger, 1960.

16. George Kennan. *Russia and the West*. New York, Atlantic-Little Brown, 1960-61.

Marx remarked in one of his *Theses on Feuerbach* (a German "theologian" whose name, if not his work, rates more than passing interest in the development of Marx's materialism) that while some people seek merely to *understand* the world, they — the Communists — intend to *change* it. This useful distinction is not in itself Marxist. Turning the world upside down was attributed to disciples earlier than those of Karl Marx. If those other disciples had been more true to their own calling in the centuries following the Renaissance, say, Karl Marx might have been unnecessary. In fact, he might have been one of them! What a speculation: Marx, Engels, Lenin, Trotsky pouring out in the service of the true Lord their matchless genius for turning worlds upside down! Instead, the Lord had to use them to teach His own would-be disciples that they were a little laggard, to say no more.

Anyhow, Marx aimed at using knowledge for action, and pointed up once again the abiding gulf between those who seek learning for possession and those who seek it for use. And in due season came the "proof of the pudding" — a revolution! It came where Marx least expected it, and in a manner not predicted for it. But it came; and now the only way the Marxist who once accepted Marx's views because he accepted Marx's hope for heaven-on-earth can still accept that hope, is by denying that what happened in Russia is the logical and inevitable conclusion from Marx's premises. Can one be a Marxist and not go down the road of brutalizing terror, moving steadily farther and farther from the dream with which Marxism first attracts its devotees? The Russian (and Chinese) experiment gives but one answer: NO! For Russia is not a Marxist deviation; it is a Marxist necessity: if man has to save himself he will destroy his neighbor in the attempt. We live in that time when Marx's "change" has been wrought; that the result is so far from what he hoped is the measure of his own misapprehension of what he believed and taught. Countless Marxists, recognizing soon or late that Russia is the nadir and desolation of their aspirations for social justice, have left the Communist Party in anguished disillusionment. What these ask of *us* now is what "change" in the world our profession of Christianity produces; for that distinction between knowledge (of God) for *understanding* and knowledge (of God) for *use* in turning a corrupt world upside down is not undone. They hear what we *say* — Marx probably knew theology from his friend Bruno Baur better than most laymen — but they want to know what we *do*, and *intend* to do, about the social problems that drove them to Marxism in the first place. Well, what do we?

So the theory came out of the books and into history, in Russia, in 1917. How it made that passage from book to deed cannot better be told than Wolfe does it in number 12 — all the more incredible because it is true. If one's taste runs to detective fiction, and if he can hardly put down the miserable thing until the plot is dissolved, he may find himself reading through to the gray light of dawn in this tale of plots and counterplots which brought the world to its present agony. There is the chapter on the Russian police spy, Malinovsky, who wormed his way so securely into Lenin's confidence that he knew the inmost secrets of the plotters, indeed was entrusted with carrying out some of them! And there was the endless infighting . . . but try it yourself! The path to Marxist paradise, like the paradise itself, was thick with intrigue and sometimes ran with blood.

Wolfe stops in 1917. No matter, for now one of the two chief actors on that gigantic stage, one sixth of the globe's surface, takes up the story himself, and leaves behind him three volumes that rank already with the Hundred Great Books and always will. After you read Trotsky, most histories will seem boundlessly uninspired, other irony will show a duller edge, other magnificent generalizations will have a lesser range and suggestiveness, the pace of other tellers of tales (true or imaginary) will seem uncommonly slow. Hardly so much a *history* as a *philosophy* of history woven around historical events, this book is dwarfed only by the deeds it recounts. Whether Trotsky could be objective at all, and whether his accuracy is unimpeachable can be endlessly debated. He can be checked by other histories, but in terms of its purposes, his is not likely to be equalled.

One check on Trotsky, though in fact written through friendly eyes and commended by Trotsky himself, is John Reed's *Ten Days*, an eye-witness account of those hectic ten days in the fall of 1917 when the power was shifting to the hands stretched forth by Lenin and Trotsky to seize it. This book, too, has the lineaments of a classic, but you will want to continue the story at once with Ambassador Kennan's masterful, knowledgeable, and incisive study. This book is not only one of the latest upon its subject, but surely the most authoritative. You might supplement it by Seton-Watson. Especially with Mr. Kennan's critique, we are now full into a critical evaluation of those changes Marxism hath made on the surface of the globe. The picture is not nice, but it is instructive, and a warning!

COMMUNISM IN AMERICA

A film or two, and a course of lectures or pamphlets are not the best guides either to Communism itself or to its threat to ourselves. If they arouse our interest and stimulate our study, they serve well; if we are led to suppose that now Communism is our oyster — as the phrase goes — they have misled us. An emotional binge is not competent anti-Communism.

There are competent guides to the Communists in America:

17. J. Edgar Hoover. *Masters of Deceit.* New York, Pocket Books, Inc.

18. M. Ernest, & D. Loth. *Report on the American Communist.* New York, Holt, 1952.

Mr. Hoover writes with the authority which is his earned right, and with the discretion born of lengthy experience with this powerful and subtle adversary. He offers not only a sketch of the apparatus, but also of the ex-Communist, who is more fully described in number 18, where the story of some three hundred former Communists is analyzed. Mr. Hoover adds a useful glossary and brief notes on major Communist classics. The book is a tribute to the man whose administration of the police power of a modern state cannot be sufficiently lauded. Start your anti-Communism from this, and be thankful for the F.B.I.

ANTI-COMMUNISM

Marxism has exercised a magnetic attraction upon many gifted persons keenly sensitive to social problems. It is an indictment of Christians not lightly to be dismissed that men and women dedicated to the amelioration of human suffering in all its forms were attracted more by Marxism than by Christianity in action. And when those gifted ones found that the promise of Marxism was grotesquely false, those who could write exposed their disillusion in memorable words. You must not miss what is in many respects the most telling and devastating indictment of Communism anywhere to be found:

19. Richard Crossman, editor. *The God that Failed.* New York, Bantam Books, Inc.

20. Howard Fast. *The Naked God.* New York, Praeger, 1957.

Perhaps you will want also to read the indictment in the form of the novel: Koestler's *Darkness at Noon* (New York, New American Library) and *The Yogi and the Commissar,* or Orwell's *Animal Farm* and *1984* (both published in New York by New American Library), or Huxley's *Brave New World,* and the later, *Brave New World Revisited* (both published in New York by Bantam Books), though none of these pricks with such awful certainty the illusions of the *Communist Manifesto* as do Koestler's, Silone's, and Wright's essays in number 19, and Fast's convulsive number 20.

CHRISTIANITY AND COMMUNISM

If not Communism, what then for those who believe the world needs changing to make it better than it is? Don't let us answer too glibly lest we be held responsible for our words.

But the answer is not secular liberalism, obviously, for Marx himself grew up and out of this. That after Adam Smith came Marx is no tribute to Smith, and a warning to those who want to return to his *laissez faire.* Nor is the answer some form of philosophical idealism, even that which substitutes contemplation of the Idea, in one form or another, for conduct. For the world moves on while the contemplatives watch or debate, and it leaves them behind if not in the lurch. Nor is the answer some form of historicism which pleads inability to alter a present because it is bound by a past. None of these, though all are tried and some are advertised.

The answer stares out at us from the titles the ex-Communists choose to summarize their own disappointment: their god has failed. Because he was not really God at all, although he wore the garments and spoke the language of a liberator. What men need is a God who fails not. That a false and empty god could evoke such a devotion and a sacrifice indisputable and awesome is a living witness to the longing of the human heart for its true Maker. Let this be *said,* then; and equally important, as Pope Pius XI said, let it be *lived* by those who teach it. ⌐

For Christian doctrine was being taught in Marx's time, and in Lenin's. But the society they saw exhibited too few signs of the redeeming power of that doctrine. There is something of the inevitable about the relation between the preaching and the practicing of any doctrine. After Leon Trotsky broke with Stalin and was expelled from Russia, it was not a question *if* the assassin would come to kill him; it was only a question *when* he would come. And he came, and Trotsky is dead. Again, when men seek to establish a society based upon the denial of God and God-based human rights, it is not a question *if* this society must become a dictatorship; it is only a question *when* it becomes one, and how ruthless that dictatorship will be. And Russia has become such a dictatorship, the most systematically ruthless in all history; and many, many more than Trotsky are dead. And again, the relation still holds: if a highly developed theoretical Christianity ignores the *double* injunction of the Law, seeking to love God and to avoid man, it is not a question *if* this hypocrisy will be found out; it is only a question of how long the process will take, and what forms of retribution time will exact.

We may expose Communism until its very bones waste away under our critique, but if our own Christianity has no effect upon the society in which we live, what will it profit us to gain the whole world from under the Communist nose? We are *against* Communism! Good! So are many ex-Communists! But what are we *for?*

This matter of the polar contest between Christianity and Communism is best explored, I think, by:

21. Jacques Maritain. *True Humanism.* London, Bles, 1946.

Professor Maritain provides some clear insight into the demands for a positive Christian approach to the modern era, though all of his conclusions should not go unmodified.

There are a great many useful books on this confrontation of the true God and the false, among them:

22. John C. Bennett. *Christianity and Communism Today.* New York, Association, 1960. This is a revision of his *Christianity and Communism* published in 1948.

The latest Catholic critique is:

23. Henri Chambre. *Christianity and Communism*. New York, Hawthorne, 1960 (Volume 96 of the 20*th* *Century Encyclopedia of Catholicism*).

A CHRISTIAN SOCIETY

But if Christianity is also concerned with changing as well as with understanding the world, what is its program? This opens a wide area of discussion, and impinges upon our task in our time. The thought of Calvin has received fluent and compre-hensive exposition in a title unfortunately not yet translated into English:

24. Henri Bieler. *La Pensée Economique et Sociale de Calvin*. Georg, 1959.

The Catholic position, ably expounded by Maritain, receives its definition in the famous encyclicals (re-affirmed by Pope John in *Mater et Magistra*, 1961) *Rerum Novarum* (1891) and *Quadragesimo Anno* (1931).

Archbishop William Temple, who frequently addressed him-self to the social implications of Christianity, summarized his views in:

25. *Christianity and Social Order*. London, Penguin Books, 1942.

There is no logical reason for stopping with twenty-five titles. Nor need you. But the understanding of these will go a long way to satisfying that "duty" Mr. Hoover writes of. And that is something.

If in addition Christian men and women of all denominations and all lands join hands for the realization of Christianity-in-society, thankful for what is now done in His name and deter-mined that ever more shall be done — that is everything!

Study, then, to drive out the bad and bring in goodness among men, asking wisdom from on high, and courage, and devotion.

BIBLIOGRAPHY

This bibliography *does not* include titles discussed in Chapter Seven.

The range of the literature in any one language is so enormous that even a much longer list would be but a selection. So brief a compilation as this is certain to omit very valuable references either unknown to or otherwise ignored by the writer. I have only included books which have been of use to me in one way or another, and have tried to group them into rough categories as indicated.

It is said that of the several thousand books in English on the life of Abraham Lincoln, not even a hundred are worthy of their subject. The problem is, of course, to determine which ones comprise the hundred-minus.

The author who speaks to you may play the sphinx to me, and for this reason every student must finally compile his own bibliography in the subjects that interest him. This is the best claim that the following list can make for its own selection.

MARX AND MARXISM

1. Marx, Karl. *Capital.* Chicago, Encyclopedia Britannica, 1952. (Also in Random House's Modern Library Giants)
2. Marx, Karl. *Communist Manifesto.* New York, International, 1948.
3. Marx, Karl. *Critique of the Gotha Programme.* New York, International, 1938.
4. Marx, Karl. *The Eighteenth Brumaire of Louis Bonaparte.* Chicago Kerr, 1914.
5. Marx, Karl. *Revolution and Counter-revolution, or Germany in 1848.* Chicago, Kerr, 1914.
6. Marx, Karl. *Value, Price and Profit.* Chicago, Kerr, n.d.

* * * * * *

7. Bouquet, Alan. *Karl Marx and His Doctrines.* London, S.P.C.K., 1952.
8. Carr, Edward. *Karl Marx. A Study in Fanaticism.* London, Dent, 1934.
9. Lindsay, A. D. *Karl Marx's Capital, an Introductory Essay.* London, Oxford University Press, 1925.
10. Mayo, Henry. *Introduction to Marxist Theory.* New York, Oxford University Press, 1960.

* * * * * *

11. Engels, Friedrich. *Feuerbach, the Roots of Socialist Philosophy.* Chicago, Kerr, 1903.
12. Engels, Friedrich. *Socialism, Utopian and Scientific.* Chicago, Kerr, 1900.
13. Lenin, Vladimir. *Imperialism.* New York, Vanguard, 1927.
14. Lenin, Vladimir. *The Teachings of Karl Marx.* New York, International, 1930.

* * * * * *

15. Meyer, Alfred. *Leninism.* Cambridge, Harvard University Press, 1957.
16. Shub, David. *Lenin.* New York, New American Library, 1950.

* * * * * *

17. Trotsky, Leon. *Literature and Revolution.* New York, Russell, 1957.

18. Trotsky, Leon. *Stalin.* New York, Harper, 1941.
19. Trotsky, Leon. *Trotsky's Diary in Exile.* Cambridge, Harvard University Press, 1935.

*   *   *   *   *   *

20. Deutscher, Isaac. *The Prophet Armed, Trotsky: 1879-1921.* London, Oxford University Press, 1954.
21. Deutscher, Isaac. *The Prophet Unarmed, Trotsky: 1921-1929.* London, Oxford University Press, 1959.

*   *   *   *   *   *

22. Fisher, Marguerite, ed. *Communist Doctrines and the Free World.* New York, Syracuse University Press, 1952.

COMMUNIST THEORY AND PRACTICE

23. Armstrong, John. *The Politics of Totalitarianism.* New York, Random House, 1961.
24. Boyer, Charles, ed. *The Philosophy of Communism.* New York, Fordham University Press, 1952.
25. Burns, Emile. *A Handbook of Marxism.* London, Gollanz, n.d.
26. Cole, G.D.H. *A History of Socialist Thought.* London, Macmillan, 1953-58 (four volumes in six).
27. Cornforth, Maurice. *Dialectical Materialism.* London, Lawrence, 1952.
28. De Man, Henry. *The Psychology of Socialism.* London, Allen & Unwin, 1928.
29. Djilas, Milovan. *The New Class.* New York, Praeger, 1957.
30. Djilas, Milovan. *Anatomy of a Moral.* New York, Praeger, 1959.
31. Fisher, Harold. *The Communist Revolution.* Stanford, Stanford University Press, 1955.
32. Hunt, Robert. *Marxism, Past and Present.* New York, Macmillan, 1955.
33. Jay, Douglas. *The Socialist Case.* London, Faber, 1938.
34. Johnson, Hewlett. *The Soviet Power.* New York, International, 1941.
35. Macek, Joseph. *The Impact of Marxism.* Pittsburgh, University of Pittsburgh Press, 1955.
36. Marcusse, Herbert. *Reason and Revolution.* New York, Humanities, 1954.
37. Meyer, Alfred. *Communism.* New York, Random House, 1960.
38. Northrop, Filmer S. C. *The Meeting of East and West.* New York, Macmillan, 1946.
39. Popper, Karl. *The Open Society and Its Enemies.* London, Routledge, 1952.
40. Rogers, Edward. *A Commentary on Communism.* London, Epworth, 1952.
41. Sprigg, Christopher St. John. *Studies in a Dying Culture.* London, Lane, 1938 (Pseudonym: Christopher Caudwell)
42. Strachey, John. *The Coming Struggle for Power.* New York, Covici Friede, 1933.
43. Sweezy, Paul. *The Theory of Capitalist Development.* London, Dobson, 1942.

CHRISTIANITY AND SOCIAL THEORY

44. Binyon, Gilbert. *The Christian Social Movement in England.* London, S.P.C.K., 1931.

45. Brunner, Heinrich Emil. *Christianity and Civilization.* London, Nisbet, 1949 (Part Two: Specific Problems).
46. Brunner, Heinrich Emil. *Communism, Capitalism, and Christianity.* London, Lutterworth, 1949.
47. Brunner, Heinrich Emil. *The Divine Imperative.* London, Lutterworth, 1937.
48. D'Arcy, Martin. *Communism and Christianity.* London, Penguin, 1956.
49. Demant, V. A. *Religion and the Decline of Capitalism.* London, Faber, 1952.
50. Eliot, Thomas S. *The Idea of a Christian Society.* London, Faber, 1939.
51. Fletcher, Joseph. *Christianity and Property.* Philadelphia, Westminster, 1947.
52. Gilson, Etienne, ed. *The Church Speaks to the Modern World; the Social Teachings of Leo XIII.* New York, Doubleday, 1954.
53. Grace, Frank. *The Concept of Property in Modern Christian Thought.* Urbana: University of Illinois Press, 1953.
54. Hordern, William. *Christianity, Communism, and History.* Nashville, Abingdon, 1954.
55. Hughes, John. *The Church and the Liberal Society.* Princeton University Press, 1944.
56. Jones, Eli Stanley. *Christ's Alternative to Communism.* New York, Abingdon, 1935.
57. Knight, F. & Merriam, T. *The Economic Order and Religion.* New York, Harper, 1945.
58. Kuyper, Abraham. *Christianity and the Class Struggle.* Grand Rapids, Piet Hein, 1950.
59. Lindsay, A. D. *Christianity and Economics.* London, Macmillan, 1933.
60. MacKinnon, Donald. *Christian Faith and Communist Faith.* London, Macmillan, 1953.
61. *Malvern, 1941.* London, Longman's, 1941.
62. Maritain, Jacques. *Christianity and Democracy.* New York, Scribner's, 1944.
63. Maritain, Jacques. *The Rights of Man.* New York, Scribner's, 1943.
64. Nitti, Francesco. *Catholic Socialism.* London, Sonnenschein, 1908.
65. Niebuhr, Reinhold. *An Interpretation of Christian Ethics.* London, S.C.M., 1936.
66. Niebuhr, Reinhold. *Faith and History.* New York, Scribner's, 1948.
67. Peck, William. *A Christian Economy.* London, S.P.C.K., 1954.
68. Rolston, Holmes. *Stewardship in the New Testament Church.* Richmond, John Knox Press, 1946.
69. Scarlett, William, ed. *The Christian Demand for Social Justice.* New York, New American Library, 1949.
70. Sheed, Francis. *Communism and Man.* New York, Sheed & Ward, 1949.
71. Sheen, Fulton. *Communism and the Conscience of the West.* New York, Garden City, 1948.
72. Tawney, R. H. *Religion and the Rise of Capitalism.* New York, New American Library, 1947.
73. Temple, William. *The Hope of a New World.* London, S.C.M., 1941.

74. Troeltsch, Ernst. *The Social Teaching of the Christian Churches.* New York, Macmillan, 1931.
75. Weber, Max. *The Protestant Ethic and the Spirit of Capitalism.* London, Allen & Unwin, 1930.
76. West, Charles C. *Communism and the Theologians.* Philadelphia, Westminster, 1958.
77. Williams, Melvin. *Catholic Social Thought.* New York, Ronald, 1950.
78. Wood, Herbert. *Christianity and Communism.* New York, Round Table, 1933.

Auxiliary

79. Beard, Charles. *The Economic Basis of Politics.* New York, Knopf, 1923.
80. Bohatec, Joseph. *Budé and Calvin.* Graz, 1950.
81. Chambers, Whittaker. *Witness.* New York, Random House, 1952.
82. Marcel, Gabriel. *Men versus Humanity.* London, Harvill, 1952.
83. Nelson, Benjamin. *The Idea of Usury.* Princeton University Press, 1949.
84. Rogers, James. *Work and Wages.* London, Sonnenschein, 1895.
85. Sabine, George. *A History of Political Theory.* New York, Holt, 1959.
86. Solovyof, Vladmir. *The Justification of the Good.* London, Constable, 1918.

SUPPLEMENTARY BIBLIOGRAPHY

For the reader who wishes to pursue a more detailed study of Marxism, the following volumes, available in the United States, will be useful:

1. Marx & Engels Selected Works in Two Volumes. Moscow, Foreign Languages Publishing House, 1958. A comprehensive selection, thoroughly indexed, in some 1,200 pages.
2. Engels, F. *Anti-Dühring.* Moscow, F.L.P.H., 1959. Engels' most extensive exposition of dialectical materialism.
3. Engels, F. *Dialectic of Nature.* Moscow, F.L.P.H., 1954. A compilation of articles on physical science.
4. Engels, F. *Ludwig Feuerbach and the End of Classical German Philosophy.* With this, one can profitably read Feuerbach's *Essence of Christianity,* available in paper cover as Harper Torchbook No. 11. Feuerbach is the bridge from Hegel to Marx; and of Hegel, Engels recommends reading the *Shorter Logic.*
5. Lenin, V. I. *Materialism and Empirico-Criticism.* Moscow, F.L.P.H. n.d. His most systematic exposition of dialectical materialism; written as a critique of certain Marxist "deviationists."
6. *Reminiscences of Marx & Engels.* Moscow, F.L.P.H. n.d. An invaluable source of personal insights and memories.
7. Krupskaya, N.K. *Lenin.* Moscow, F.L.P.H., 1959. Memoirs of Lenin by his wife.
8. Trotsky, L. *My Life.* Grosset & Dunlap paperback, 1960.

A new three-volume edition of Marx's *Capital* is also published by Moscow, from the third German edition translated by Moore and Aveling: F.L.P.H., 1961.

INDEX OF SUBJECTS

Agricultural surplus, Christian view of   115-7
Alienation   32
Anti-Communism, Christian   119ff.
Bonapartism,   46
Bourgeoisie
  defined,   13
  Marxist use of term Bourgeois,   73
  Marxist view of role in history,   95
Capitalism
  basic premises of,   36-8
  laissez faire modified,   103
  manner of defence of,   38
  Marxist response to,   37-8
  results of,   101
  strengths of,   38
Class struggle
  Christian interpretation of,   112
  Marxist view of,   22-5, 98
Classless society
  defined,   34
  Communist heaven: *see* Salvation
  criticism of Marxist view of, 47-51, 60-1, 64-8
Communism
  meaning summed up by Engels, 11
  meaning summed up by Marx, 12, 35
Communist Manifesto,   4, 8
Declaration of Independence,   4
Declaration of the Rights of man, French,   4, 131
Demonic
  in Marxism,   92-7
  as real enemy,   129-33
Democracy
  Calvin on,   101
  Capitalism and,   38
Dialectical materialism
  basic assumptions of,   83

covert idealism in,   97
defined,   28-30
in classless society,   97
role of negation in,   94-7
see also: Economic determinism
Economic determinism
  of human conduct,   82
  of education,   26, 108-9
  of religion,   27, 109
  of the state,   25, 109
Education
  Christian,   40, 113-4
  economic determination of,   26, 108-9
Evil
  Christian conception of,   52
  Marxist conception of, 43, 71, 77-81
  Marxist holds bourgeoisie responsible for,   74-5
  see also: Salvation
Evolutionary optimism
  Marxist use of,   78
  Adam Smith's use of,   106-7
Faith and works: *see* Understanding and action
Freedom
  and choice of evil, in Marxism, 78-80
  and ideals,   90-1
  and necessity,   86, 91
  and property,   55-6
  Christian conception of,   84-5
  Lenin as illustration of,   87-9
  Marx's definition of,   84
Hedonism
  in Adam Smith,   105
  in Jeremy Bentham,   107
History
  and eternity: *see* Judgment
  Christian conception of, 68-9, 72,

111, 131, 137
defined,   63-4
dynamic of,   1, 92-97, 131
Marxist philosophy of, 27-8, 33-4,
    64-6, 86
Humanism
    as anti-Communist,   119-20, 132
    in education,   124
Incarnation,   139
Imperialism, Lenin's view of,   32
Industrial revolution, consequences
    of,   12
Judgment, Christian doctrine of,
    109-11
Labor, socially necessary,   15-6
Labor value
    Christian interpretation of,   102
    Marxist conception of,   14-6, 102
Liberalism, economic
    Christian judgment upon,   109-118
    classical view, in Marxism,   103-7
    enlightened self-interest in,   26
    evils mitigated by social legisla-
        tion,   107-8
    led to Marxism,   107
    see also: Capitalism
Love for enemies, Christian,   133-5
Lying,   124
Man, Christian conception of, 51-3,
    91
    see also: Evolutionary optimism
Marx, Karl
    birth 7, education 7, reporter and
    editor 8, marries Jenny von West-
    phalen 8, exiled 8, meets Engels 8,
    settles in London 8, mathematician
    8, writes Capital 9, poverty 9,
    family life 9, organizes First Inter-
    national 10, death 10, lessons of
    his life, 10
Marxism, right and left,   34
Materialism, see Dialectical material-
    ism
Morality, Communist,   33, 45, 85
    see also: Freedom
Mystery, Christian conception of,
    85, 91
Negation, Marxist use of,   94-7
Pacificism,   132-3, 135-6
Paradox, Christian conception of, 63,
    80, 111

Party Line, Communist,   73-5
Perfectionism
    abstract standard in Marxism, 38,
    77
    Christian view of,   100-1
    see also: Utopianism
Power
    struggle for in Communist nations,
    45
    source of in history,   92-7, 131
Profit, Marxist conception of, 19-21,
    29
Proletariat
    dictatorship of,   32-4
    law of increasing misery of, 31, 101
    Marxist conception of,   13, 24
    negative role in history,   95
    positive role in history,   96
    private property and,   57
    real misery of,   61
Property
    Christian conception of, 55-7, 59-60
    private ownership of,   30
    root of evil, Marxist and Christian
    views,   42, 80
Revisionism,   35
Rheinische Zeitung, Marx on staff
    of,   8
    Neue Rheinishce Zeitung, Marx
    edits,   9
Revelation, Biblical   69
Revolution, Marxist view of,   31-2
    see also: Salvation
Roman Catholic encyclicals on labor,
    114
Russian Revolution, Lenin's role in,
    87-9
Salvation
    Christian conception of,   52, 67
    evaluation of Marxist conception
    of,   47-51
    man as making own, in Marxism,
    77-81
    Marxist conception of,   44, 66-8
    parallels between Christian and
    Marxist,   53, 67
Secularism,   119-20
Self-examination
    Church challenged by Marxism to,
    127-9
    Communist threat implies,   124-5

refusal dangerous, 126
total, 125
Self-realization
    frustrated in Marxism, 86
    realized in Christianity, 86
Social legislation, role of, 107-9
Society, Christian doctrine of, 54
Stalinism, implied in Marxism, 45-7
State
    and economic life, 40, 107-8
    withering away of, 34
    see also: Social legislation
Stewardship
    Christian doctrine of, 57-62, 118
    national, of food surplus, 115-7
Surplus value
    Christian interpretation of, 102, 112
    Marxist conception of, 16-20

Theology of Marxism, 41-2
Time: see History
Truth, Christian obligation to, 121-4
Understanding
    as end in itself, 2
    as means, 3
    relation to action in Christianity, 85, 115, 132
    relation to action in Marxism, 115
Utopianism
    basis of Marxist critique of history, 70-1
    basis of Marxist irresponsibility, 74
    removes classless society from critique 69
Wages, Marxist view of, 20-1
War, 131-3
Words, 123
    see also: Humanism

INDEX OF PROPER NAMES

Adams, H., 105
Adler, M., 121
Augustine, Saint, 58, 94, 96
Barth, K., 98
Bentham, J., 107
Berdyaev, N., 3
Bernstein, E., 35
Browning, R., 12
Brunner, E., 98
Cabanis, P., 88
Calvin, J., 20, 55, 68, 94, 101, 120, 121, 124, 125, 133
Chambers, W., 96
Chambre, P., 115
Churchill, W. S., 88
Cornforth, M., 74
Darwin, C., 63
Demonsthenes, 121
Descartes, R., 60
Donne, J., 135
Dostoevsky, F., 51, 132
Duchess of Ferrara, 133
Edwards, J., 58
Eliot, G. (pseud.), 110
Emerson, R. W., 74

Engels, F., 8, 9, 10, 11, 12, 21, 24, 28, 69, 70, 71, 79, 86, 95, 98
Fast, H., 47
Feuerbach, L., 32
Franklin, B., 16
Goethe, J. W. von, 11
Greeley, H., 9
Hegel, G. W. F., 28, 29, 35, 63, 94, 95, 98
Hess, M., 9
Hook, S., 35
Hoover, J. E., 140
James, W., 90, 115
Jesus Christ, 52, 57, 58, 61, 62, 69, 85, 93, 109, 110, 113, 114, 118, 119, 133
Kautsky, K., 9, 35
Keynes, J. M., 109
Khrushchev, N., 46, 125
Kingsley, C., 71
Koestler, A., 35
Kuyper, A., 54
LaPlace, P., 3
Lenin, N., 32, 33, 34, 35, 46, 48, 64, 73, 74, 87, 88, 89, 96, 98

Lewis, C. S.,   58, 125
Locke, J.,   16
Ludlow, J. M.,   71
Malthus, R.,   15, 17, 21, 26
Marcel, G.,   85
Maritain, J.,   61, 62, 94, 95, 114
Marshall, A.,   109
Martineau, J.,   90
Marx, K., 1, 2, 7, 8, 9, 10, 11, 12,
   13, 14, 15, 16, 19, 20, 21, 24, 25,
   27, 28, 29, 30, 31, 32, 33, 34, 35,
   37, 42, 43, 44, 45, 47, 48, 49, 51,
   52, 53, 55, 56, 57, 59, 60, 64, 65,
   69, 70, 71, 76, 77, 78, 79, 80, 81,
   82, 83, 84, 86, 90, 91, 95, 97, 98, 100,
   101, 102, 105, 106, 107, 108, 113,
   114, 116, 117, 118, 120, 139
Maurice, F. W.,   71
Napoleon,   132
Nebuchadnezzar,   125
Ortega y Gasset, J.,   105
Owen, R.,   30
Pope Leo XIII,   114
Pope Pius XI,   58, 114

Ricardo, D., 15, 16, 17, 20, 21, 27,
   107
Rip van Winkle,   138
Rousseau, J. J.,   48
Saint James,   56, 132
Saint Paul, 52, 57, 68, 80, 93, 94,
   109, 111, 131
Satan,   93, 124, 130, 139
Schlesinger, R.,   90
Smith, A., 12, 13, 16, 17, 21, 26, 103,
   104, 105, 106, 107, 108, 109, 113,
   114, 116, 118, 121
Solovyof, V. S.,   128, 129, 135
Stalin, J.,   46, 64, 65, 114
Temple, W.,   55
Thomas Aquinas,   18
Thompson, F.,   52
Thorez, M.,   114
Thornton, L. S.,   85, 90
Toynbee, A.,   123
Trotsky, L., 3, 11, 46, 65, 87, 88, 89,
   90, 114, 120, 132
Victoria, Queen,   22
Von Westphalen, J.,   8, 10, 11

INDEX OF SCRIPTURE

Exodus   20:15   112
              20:16   112, 124
Joshua   24:15   118
Psalm   34:8   85
Ecclesiastes 12:14   110
Isaiah   7:7   3
Matthew   6:33   112
              7:5   125
              7:9   53
              7:12   112
              11:28   99, 118
              12:36   110
              16:26   60
Mark   8:36   61
Luke   9:54   129
              10:17-20   113
              11:11   53
              12:5   58
              12:8   111-2
              12:31   61
              19:40   54

John   8:44   124
              14:23   85
Romans   7:24   94
              7:25   85
              8:22   53
              8:39   52
              12:20   134
I Corinthians 1:23-24   93
              3:22   61-2
              12:4-13   57
              13:12   63, 80
              15:20   109
              15:41   68
              15:53-4   110
Galatians   6:7   58, 68
Ephesians   2:9   111
              6:12   93, 131
Philippians   2:12   111
I Timothy   6:10   80
James   2:17   132
              2:20   62